LATIN MIGRATION NORTH

LATIN MIGRATION NORTH

The Problem for U.S. Foreign Policy

MICHAEL S. TEITELBAUM

Council on Foreign Relations

COUNCIL ON FOREIGN RELATIONS BOOKS

Library of Congress Cataloging in Publication Data

Teitelbaum, Michael S.
    Latin migration north.

    Bibliography: p.
    1. United States--Emigration and immigration--
Government policy. 2. Latin America--Emigration and
immigration. 3. United States--Foreign relations--
Latin America. 4. Latin America--Foreign relations--
United States. I. Title.
JV6483.T45 1985   325'.28'0973   85-11322
ISBN 0-87609-007-2 (pbk.)

Contents

The author wishes to thank Diego C. Asencio, Carl Hampe, Marion F. Houstoun, Paul H. Kreisberg, Susan Kaufman Purcell, William D. Rogers and Daniel A. Sharp and all the members of the Council's Study Group, listed on page 78, for their constructive comments, and Rob Valkenier and David Kellogg for assistance in the production of this book. He is also grateful for an earlier opportunity to serve as Senior Associate of the Carnegie Endowment for International Peace, which allowed him to focus seriously upon the broad connections between immigration/refugee issues and foreign policy.

Foreword

The United States has reached a crucial point in its debate over immigration policy. Several years of sometimes impassioned discussion have resulted in two unsuccessful attempts by Congress to pass a series of reforms known as the Simpson-Mazzoli bills. The issue of immigration reform is, however, far from dead; it seems certain that a revised version of the legislation will receive serious Congressional consideration in 1985. *Latin Migration North: The Problem for U.S. Foreign Policy* is intended as an impartial contribution to help resolve the current impasse over immigration policy.

Since the 1960s it has been apparent that our immigration policy and our foreign policy affect one another both directly and indirectly. Yet immigration policy has traditionally been treated by policy makers and scholars primarily as a domestic issue. The ways in which foreign and domestic considerations and interests interact in the area of immigration remained unclear and in need of systematic study.

In 1982 the Council on Foreign Relations decided to devote attention to the immigration issue by organizing a study group on Latin American Immigration and U.S. Foreign Policy. The relevance of the study group and of its focus on Latin America was reinforced by the growing national debate over the rapid increase in illegal aliens entering and remaining in the United States from the Western Hemisphere, particularly Mexico and the Caribbean Basin, as well as by the mounting calls for significant reform of U.S. immigration laws. Furthermore, the debt crisis and the volatile situation in Central America highlighted the need to address the immigration issue in the broader context of U.S. foreign policy toward Latin America. At the same time, it was obvious that the study could not be limited solely to the relationship between Latin American migration and U.S. policy toward the region, but instead would have to place the Latin American case within a broader discussion of immigration and U.S. foreign policy.

The Council's study group, which met ten times between March 1982 and 1984, included leading U.S. experts on immigration and refugee issues and individuals with wide experience and background in Latin America and the Caribbean. Its thorough deliberations as well as the information and insights contained in working papers commissioned by the group are drawn upon extensively in Michael Teitelbaum's thoughtful treatment of the issues. As intended, however, the following pages reflect the views of the author, not necessarily those of the study group or its members. Because of the diversity of viewpoints represented, no consensus statement was even contemplated.

Latin Migration North: The Problem for U.S. Foreign Policy is the first publication of the Council's Latin American Project, which was established in 1982. The Council wishes to thank the funders of the Latin American Project, whose generosity made this study possible. They include the Andrew W. Mellon Foundation, the Tinker Foundation, the Ford Foundation, Xerox Corporation, the Grace Foundation, IBM/World Trade Americas/Far East Corporation, the Chase Manhattan Bank and the General Electric Company. The Council wishes to thank as well the members of the Latin American Immigration and Foreign Policy study group for giving generously, over a period of nearly two years, their vast expertise, time and effort.

Daniel A. Sharp
Study Group Chairman

Susan Kaufman Purcell
Director, Latin American Program

Paul H. Kreisberg
Director of Studies

1

Introduction

Immigration issues have become as disturbing and divisive as any problem on the contemporary American scene. They challenge law-makers and law-enforcers, churches and chambers of commerce, politicians and academics. Immigration today is heavily economic, yet at the same time quintessentially political. In unpredictable and sometimes bizarre ways, it realigns, allies, and divides Northeasterners and Southwesterners, Democrats and Republicans, liberals and conservatives, business and labor, whites and nonwhites, foreign-born and native-born. The importance, urgency and difficulty of the issues have been amply demonstrated in more than three years of indecisive congressional debate on the Immigration Reform and Control Act, also known as the Simpson-Mazzoli bill.

Though often seen in solely domestic terms, immigration and refugee issues in reality raise complex domestic problems enveloped in a mantle of vexing foreign policy dilemmas. The causal relationships between immigration/refugee issues and foreign policy concerns run in both directions: foreign policies have both stimulated and restrained international migrations; and migrations, in turn, have had significant effects on foreign policy.

In the recent past, such effects have been far more important than was generally perceived, and in the foreseeable future they show every sign of intensifying. In the same way that crises in economics, energy supply, and terrorism rose to international prominence in the 1970s, so immigration and refugee issues have now become critical issues in foreign affairs. In the United States of the 1980s, no foreign policy maker can safely ignore the questions raised by mass movements of people across international borders.

The inextricable connections between U.S. foreign policy and international migrations have been especially evident in migrations from Latin America to the United States over the last three decades, which are for this country the largest, the most urgent, and the most controversial. The foreign and domestic questions they raise are profound ones:

• Is it possible to secure reasonable control over illegal immigration from Latin America and the Caribbean region without poisoning U.S.-Latin America relations and contributing to instability within the source countries?

• Should special immigration preferences be granted to Mexico (and/or other nations in the region), as an exception to the principle of equal treatment for all nations that has prevailed in U.S. immigration law since 1965?

• Has U.S. foreign or domestic policy unintentionally exacerbated pressures for Latin American and Caribbean migration to the United States? If so, can changes be made without violating other important policy principles?

• Should foreign policy considerations have any bearing on decisions concerning refugee admissions and asylum adjudications?

• Is the United States prepared to be a country of "first asylum," to which those seeking refuge can move directly in boats, planes or over land, as distinct from its recent role as a country of permanent resettlement for refugees given first asylum elsewhere?

• Is it possible to negotiate an agreement with the Cuban government that would effectively prevent repetition of the chaotic uncontrolled movement of a large number of Cubans to south Florida in 1980? If another such mass exodus were to be initiated by the Cuban government, what should be the U.S. reaction?

To consider such issues, the Council on Foreign Relations convened a carefully balanced Study Group to consider international migration in both international and domestic terms. The Group, whose membership is listed on page 78, consisted of participants with widely diverse backgrounds and perspectives on the issues, and from time to time invited additional participants, including such key congressional figures as Senator Alan K. Simpson (R-Wyoming) and Representative Romano L. Mazzoli (D-Kentucky).

The following report builds upon the discussions of that Study Group over a two-year period. From the outset it was agreed that the Study Group would not seek to reach policy consensus on issues that could be expected to defy unanimity. Instead, the agreed goal was to illuminate the issues and the available alternative policy choices. The aim of this report is to reflect the diversity of opinions, though ultimately the conclusions presented here are those of the author and not of the Study Group or of the Council on Foreign Relations.

2

Some Background

International migration is hardly a new phenomenon. Human migration has occurred since the appearance of the species several million years ago, and migration across international boundaries has taken place since the establishment of the nation-state system. Why, then, should the subject now rise to policy prominence, both domestically and in terms of U.S. relations with Latin America? The reasons are several and diverse, reflecting both long-term trends and quite recent developments.

First, the spread of the nation-state system to essentially all of the world's land mass has eliminated areas over which sovereign control was exercised by a colonial power or by no recognizable state. Migration from Europe to North or South America, or from Mexico to California, is now an international movement among sovereign nations, which it often was not in the eighteenth and nineteenth centuries.

Second, most of the sparsely populated nation-states that long welcomed and even recruited immigrants have become more developed and densely settled. By the 1980s, nearly all of these countries demonstrated their desire for the sharp curtailment of further immigration.

Third, rapid economic advance in Western countries since World War II coupled with development problems elsewhere have led to large and increasing disparities in the standard of living between Western nations and those of the Third World, thereby providing greater economic incentives for in-

12

ternational migration. This is especially true in the Americas, where wealthy and poor nations share long common borders. The outstanding example is that of the United States and Mexico—a unique case of a 2,000-mile unmilitarized border between a highly industrialized country and a Third World state.

Fourth, the number of potential international migrants has increased dramatically in the past two decades. This is a consequence of the rapid population growth that more than doubled the population of the developing world since World War II, and that is now causing an equally rapid growth in the labor force. Latin America had the most marked demographic increase of all developing regions in the 1950s and 1960s (although it has been overtaken by Africa in the last decade), and consequently faces the most rapid labor force growth during the 1980s and 1990s.

Fifth, international migration seems to be linked to urbanization, and Latin America is the urbanized developing region *par excellence*, with a long-standing urban tradition. Recent United Nations projections[1] indicate that by the year 1990 the two largest cities in the world will both be in Latin America—Mexico City and São Paulo—and that by the year 2000 these cities may contain 26 million and 24 million persons respectively, up from 1980 levels of 15 and 13 million. For perspective, the two largest urban agglomerations in 1980, Tokyo/Yokohama and New York/Northeastern New Jersey, are projected at about 17 and 16 million in the year 2000.[2]

Sixth, improvements in transportation have transformed the nature of international migrations—from long, dangerous and expensive sea journeys to quick, safe and easily available jet flights. Concurrently, improvements in international communication have brought the possibility and attractiveness of such migrations to the attention of previously isolated populations in remote areas.

The effects of these long-term trends have been amplified by developments of the past decade. The global recession of the 1970s and 1980s, stimulated in part by the steep increases in energy prices of 1973–74 and 1979–80, exacerbated economic problems in most of the developing countries, and especially in those lacking indigenous energy resources. Even energy-rich developing countries such as Mexico experienced serious economic instability, rising unemployment, and burgeoning foreign debt, leading eventually to financial crisis, devaluations, and restrictions on economic growth.

Meanwhile, in the same countries the large baby-boom generations born in the 1960s and 1970s were coming of age, causing an extraordinarily rapid growth in the labor force at a time of slow or even negative economic growth. The large birth generations of the past two decades also mean that children constitute a high percentage of these countries' populations (in many Latin American countries, 40–50 percent are under age 15), and hence that an even greater increase in the labor force is a certainty over the rest of the century.

In the Western industrialized countries, economic recession in the 1970s terminated the sustained economic-boom phase of the 1950s and 1960s, unemployment rose to record levels since the Great Depression of the 1930s, and political, economic and social stresses intensified. Although such tensions led by the 1980s to the curtailment of legal immigration in almost all of the industrialized countries (the United States was a notable exception), they remained attractive destinations for migrants from countries in which unemployment rates were even higher and wages far lower. Meanwhile, indigenous fertility and population growth in industrialized countries declined sharply from the mid-1960s onward, thereby increasing the demographic significance of immigration.

Finally, these long-term and more recent trends were brought into sharper focus by a series of new international migrations widely viewed as "crises." Some of the most visible of these occurred in Asia (e.g., the Indochinese "boat people" crisis, or the flight of millions of Afghan refugees following the Soviet intervention in Afghanistan). But at least four of the most important of these crises occurred in the Americas and necessarily seized the attention of policy makers.

1) In a six-month period during 1980, the United States experienced an uncontrolled influx of more than 125,000 Cubans,

including a minority who were violent criminals, psychotics, and terminally ill patients apparently expelled by the Castro regime. Although some 850,000 Cubans had migrated to the United States in the previous two decades following Castro's victory in Cuba, the so-called Mariel boatlift of 1980 posed new and serious problems for law enforcement and health officials in the United States. Publicity on these problems did serious damage to public perceptions of refugee issues. The persistent refusal of the Cuban government until 1984 to readmit the minority who are excludable under U.S. law erected a major barrier to improvement in Cuban-U.S. relations. In domestic terms, some observers believe that the Carter Administration's handling of the Cuban boatlift may have been an important issue in the 1980 Presidential election.

2) In 1979 and 1980, thousands of poor Haitians sought to sail to Florida beaches in small boats. In some cases their attempts ended in tragic mass drownings. Class actions and thousands of individual asylum claims filed on behalf of these migrants entangled the federal courts in a series of contradictory rulings that have still not been satisfactorally sorted out. The Haitian migration, and U.S. government reactions to it, also brought on a politically charged debate replete with charges of racial discrimination and foreign policy favoritism.

3) Meanwhile, the out-migration of large numbers of Salvadorans, Nicaraguans, and Guatemalans over the last half-decade became painfully evident as hundreds of thousands have appeared in the United States and in the border areas of neighboring countries. These migrations from a poverty-stricken and politically unstable region have served to remind governments of the relationships between their foreign policies and international migrations, as well as of the domestic dangers that such migrations may pose.

4) The economic crisis that began in Mexico in 1982 led to a massive flight of capital, a near-default on Mexico's foreign debt, and a 90-percent devaluation of the peso. The result was flat or negative economic growth, rising unemployment, large

declines in real wages, and growing wage differentials between Mexico and the United States. The effects on Mexican migration to the United States were predictable: apparent increases in illegal flows, as evidenced by sharply higher numbers of arrests without commensurate expansion of the enforcement effort.

3

Who Are the Migrants and What Are the Numbers?

In discussing international migrants, three categories must be distinguished: legal permanent immigrants, refugees, and a third grouping of more temporary migrants comprising both legal temporary workers and illegal migrants.

It is worth noting that immigrants in the traditional sense (i.e., settlers with legal rights of permanent residence) may no longer constitute the main component of international migration. Over the past decade, perhaps 10 million persons, or about one million per year, have fallen into this category. About a half of this total have migrated to a single country, the United States.

Refugees—those leaving their homelands due to "persecution" (which has a specific legal meaning different from that in normal usage, as discussed below)—may be as numerous as immigrants. The world's refugee population in need of assistance or resettlement was estimated conservatively to be about 9.1 million persons as of mid-1984, and was almost certainly larger at the beginning of 1985.[3]

Probably the largest category of international migrants today is the "temporary" grouping, numbering some 20–30 million persons. Perhaps 10–15 million have been lawfully admitted to their countries of residence for temporary stays, mostly in Western Europe and the Persian Gulf region. Another 10–15 million or so (the numbers here are very uncertain) are in an illegal or undocumented status, concentrated heavily in the Western Hemisphere (especially in the United States and Venezuela), as well as in India and a few other countries.[4] Many of these have become long-time residents despite their extralegal status.

All numerical assessments of immigration in various categories should recognize that return migration may in some cases be of significant magnitude. Estimates of immigration or refugee populations or annual "net migration flows" take explicit account of such return migration, but crude estimates of immigrant inflows need to be reduced by parallel estimates of outflows. Such outflows may be quite substantial in some cases (e.g., the inflow of illegal immigrants to the United States may well number in the millions each year, but return flows reduce the net flow substantially), and quite small in others (e.g., in the case of those political refugees who find return migration dangerous or highly undesirable). Available data on return migration are very limited, even for legal immigrants, and are particularly poor for illegal migrants. Indeed, a principal source of disagreement about the size and growth rate of the illegal alien population in the United States arises from differing assumptions as to the extent of return migration among illegal in-migrants.

The refugee category deserves elaboration here, as its differences from legal and illegal immigration are sometimes unclear and have been the subject of extensive manipulation. In the Refugee Act of 1980, the term "refugee" was changed from its previous heavily Cold War definition ("because of persecution or fear of persecution on account of race, religion, or political opinion . . . have fled from any Communist-dominated country or area, or from any country within the general area of the Middle East . . . or persons uprooted by catastrophic natural calamity as defined by the President") to one based on international law, as follows:

> any person who is outside of any country of such person's nationality . . . and who is unable or unwilling to return to, and is unable or unwilling to avail himself or herself of the protection

of, that country because of persecution or a well-founded fear of persecution on account of race, religion, nationality, membership in a particular social group, or political opinion . . . [5]

While there is no universal agreement on what constitutes "persecution," deliberate actions by governments that threaten the life or freedom of individuals on one or more of the five grounds listed surely would qualify. But those leaving their homes due to drought, flood, earthquake or other acts of God, the generalized violence of civil or international war, desperate poverty, racial or other discrimination, or any other similar circumstances not involving deliberate "persecution" would not qualify as refugees.

It will be obvious to the reader that this is an area in which legal definitions and administrative interpretations may differ significantly from those commonly used in the press and elsewhere. The differences are of critical importance, since desperate, dangerous, and unfair conditions afflict hundreds of millions of people in the world, but only a minority are qualified for the special treatment accorded refugees qualifying under the internationally agreed definition. The special treatment includes protection from forced repatriation, direct economic assistance, and preferential resettlement in third countries. These benefits are sufficiently attractive to explain the growth of manipulation and abuse of the refugee category.

In Latin America and the Caribbean region, there is much controversy over the number of persons who reside outside their homelands as legal immigrants, illegal immigrants, and refugees.[6] A recent review notes that there are serious problems with the data on legal as well as illegal immigration. For example, the United Nations *1977 Demographic Yearbook*, which included international migration as its special topic, focused only on permanent immigration in its tables. Unfortunately,

> the definitions of permanent migration used by most countries are so restrictive that almost no migrants fall into this category. In addition, few emigrants are willing to declare intent to emigrate permanently for a variety of reasons: uncertain[ty] about actual intent; a declaration would affect social security benefits

or other legal privileges; and most immigrants, even if they want to remain permanently, probably are not entering on a visa that permits anything other than work for a specific period of time or perhaps no work . . . [7]

With such limitations accepted as given (and excluding Latin American migrants to the United States, discussed separately below), it is generally agreed that several million persons currently reside as legal immigrants in nations of the Latin American region other than their homelands. The bulk of these may be found at two regional "poles"—the relatively prosperous countries of Venezuela and Argentina. Venezuela's legal alien population has been estimated at 2 million out of a 1980 population of about 17 million.[8] Argentina's foreign-born population was estimated at 534,000 in 1970, out of a population of 23.4 million.[9]

There also are at least several million undocumented migrants in Latin America, most of whom have moved to the same relatively prosperous nations. Venezuela has the largest undocumented population, estimated at some 2 million,[10] and illegal residence is "common" in rural areas of Argentina.[11] In addition, an estimated 500,000–700,000 Haitians now reside in Venezuela, Colombia, Mexico, the United States, Canada, and numerous Caribbean nations, including approximately 300,000 in the Dominican Republic and some 10 percent of the population of the Bahamas.[12]

Many hundreds of thousands of persons claiming refugee status or political asylum are to be found in the Americas, although many are not officially recognized by either their host government or the international community. For example, several hundred thousand Uruguayans and a similar number of Argentinians are thought to have departed their homelands for mainly political reasons. Some 100,000 Chileans and 18,000 nationals of other countries are reported to have left Chile at the time of the overthrow of the Allende government in 1973.

The number of Central Americans claiming refugee or asylum status is also dramatic. An estimated 300,000–500,000 Salvadorans have left their country in recent years for both economic and political reasons. Although El Salvador has for decades been a country of out-migration for largely economic reasons, some of the more recent migrants would qualify as refugees from "persecution," and others, while not qualifying as refugees, are fleeing the violence and economic disloca-tions of the Salvadoran civil war. Some 20,000 Salvadorans and 30,000 Guatemalans are registered in refugee camps in Honduras and in southern Mexico run by the United Nations High Commissioner for Refugees (UNHCR). In addition, an estimated 30,000–40,000 Nicaraguans have left the country, including some 12,000 Miskito Indians living just across the Honduras-Nicaragua border.

Caribbean island nations in recent years also have experi-enced large migrant and refugee flows. Perhaps most notable are the estimated 1 million Cubans—some 10 percent of the entire population—who have departed since 1959 for a mix-ture of political, economic and family reasons. Most of them have been admitted by the United States as refugees or Cuban "entrants."

These large-scale migrations of Latin American nationals have had major consequences for the United States, tradi-tionally a country of immigration. The United States was the classic resource-rich and labor-poor developing country of the nineteenth century, with an enormous demand for immi-grants to populate its sparsely settled frontiers and to staff its labor-short factories. Thus unlimited immigration was permit-ted by the United States government until well into the nine-teenth century. As the land mass was gradually settled and the industrial base began to mature, shortages of labor and settlers became of lesser concern, and there followed a cen-tury-long transition toward increased barriers to immigration. At first, in the 1870s, immigration was limited on qualitative grounds, and in the 1920s it was limited numerically and has been so ever since.

As a result of these gradual shifts in policy, along with altered economic and political circumstances that changed the relative attractiveness of migration to the United States, the overall numbers of legal immigrants varied substantially over time. In the 160-odd years from 1820 to 1981, some 50.3 million persons immigrated legally to the United States, with the heaviest flows occurring during the half-century from 1880 to 1930.

Legal immigration rose rapidly during the buoyant second half of the nineteenth century, peaking in the 1901–10 decade at about 880,000 legal immigrants per year.[13] It then declined sharply to an annual average of 52,800 in the 1931–40 decade and rose again only after the end of World War II. The principal countries of origin were, at different times, the United Kingdom, Ireland, Germany, Sweden, Italy, Austro-Hungary, and Russia.

Legal immigration has been increasing quite rapidly through the 1950s, 1960s, and 1970s, rising by 30 percent or more each decade. The major countries of origin have also changed dramatically, away from the prior overwhelming

Table 1. Legal Immigration to the United States, by Regions and Decades, 1941–80

	1941–50	1951–60	1961–70	1971–80
Total	1,035,039	2,515,479	3,321,677	4,493,314
Europe	621,124	1,325,640	1,123,363	800,368
Asia	32,360	150,106	427,771	1,588,178
Canada	171,718	377,952	413,310	169,939
Africa, and other	26,751	42,789	54,169	122,239
Latin America and the Caribbean	183,086	618,992	1,303,064	1,812,590
Mexico	60,589	299,811	453,937	640,294
Caribbean	49,725	123,091	470,213	741,126
Central America	21,665	44,751	101,330	134,640
South America	21,831	91,628	257,954	295,741
Other	29,276	59,711	19,630	789

Source: Calculated from Immigration and Naturalization Service, *1981 Statistical Yearbook*, Table 2.

dominance of Europe and toward the current overwhelming dominance of Latin America and Asia. By the late 1970s, fully 87 percent of legal immigrants were from regions other than Europe. Latin America and the Caribbean was the one region providing the most legal immigrants, accounting for just over 40 percent of the total. (Data for 1980 and 1981 suggest that Asia may have surpassed Latin America and the Caribbean in the number of legal immigrants in those years, though such comparisons are complicated by the delayed incorporation of earlier Asian refugee movements into the immigrant counts.)

As to individual countries of origin, Mexico is by far the largest, accounting on its own for roughly 15 percent of total legal immigrants in the 1970s. Indeed, Latin American legal migrants to the United States come overwhelmingly from the Caribbean Basin region (here defined to include Mexico, Central America and the South American nations bordering the Caribbean Sea in addition to the islands). One analysis estimates that:

> 95.9 percent of all Americas' [legal] immigrants to the United States come from the Caribbean region. This is a striking statistic when it is considered that the countries constituting "other America" . . . have about half the non-U.S. population in the Americas but contributed only 4.1 percent of legal migrants in the 1972–1976 period.[14]

Hence on this basis it is reasonable to focus our attention most heavily upon the Caribbean Basin component of legal migration from Latin America to the United States. And here, by far the largest country of origin has been Mexico (alone accounting for at least one-third of the total), followed well behind by Cuba, Jamaica, the Dominican Republic, El Salvador, Colombia, Ecuador, and Guyana.[15]

In addition to these legal immigration figures, two other components of U.S. immigration must be considered if a balanced numerical assessment is to be made. The first component is legal temporary migrant programs, such as the *bracero* program that imported some 5 million Mexican contract laborers between 1942 and 1964. During the 1970s, there was also a total of 500,000 temporary workers admitted legally under the so-called "H-visa" program, approximately 40 percent of whom were professionals or workers deemed to possess special skills.

The second component is illegal or undocumented migration. While immigration laws surely have been violated to some degree since their first adoption, the extent of such abuse has varied dramatically over time. There is clear evidence of widespread illegal immigration accompanying the *bracero* program after World War II, until a law enforcement crackdown in 1954. The 1960s do not seem to have been a period of widespread illegal immigration, but during the 1970s the phenomenon grew rapidly and appears to be increasing to the time of this writing.

The nature and implications of U.S. experiences with illegal immigration have been often exaggerated by advocates on various sides. There has, for example, been sharp disagreement as to the magnitude of the "flows" and "stocks" (or cumulative net numbers) of illegal migrants. Although a broad range of estimates have been put forward at one time or another, a "stock" estimate range of between 3.5 million and 6 million as of about 1978 seems to have gained some substantial agreement. The level of annual flows net of return migrations since then are also controversial, although few observers would object to a crude range of at least several hundred thousand but considerably less than a million.

It is hardly surprising, upon reflection, that numerical disputes have plagued the debate. Illegal immigration is (by definition) *sub rosa*, and participants in the process have little desire to be enumerated by government agencies. In short, illegal immigration is essentially inaccessible to accurate measurement, as are other clandestine phenomena such as tax evasion, drug abuse, or the "underground economy." No one can know today with any accuracy what the true size and growth rate of the illegal alien population are, nor will firm evidence ever become available. Debate on the figures can be expected to continue among the vocal advocates, for no one will be able to provide incontrovertible proof that any numerical claim is wrong.

Perhaps surprisingly, there is less disagreement as to the national origins of illegal immigrants. Although Mexican nationals comprise nearly 90 percent of U.S. Border Patrol apprehensions, it is generally agreed that Mexicans account for perhaps 50–60 percent of illegal immigrants, those from elsewhere in Latin America and the Caribbean for a further 15–25 percent, and the rest of the world for the remainder. The bulk of these appear to enter the United States unlawfully, although some (unknown) proportion are accounted for by abusers of lawful temporary visas (visitors, students, etc.).

If the numbers themselves are controversial, then the implications can hardly be less so. Various advocates express diverse judgments regarding the effects of illegal immigration upon U.S. labor markets, social services, political principles, civil rights, and intergroup relations. Unsurprisingly, those advocates who favor the current immigration regime (for example, agricultural interests in the Southwest, some Hispanic politicians and activists, some immigration and civil liberties lawyers, and some conservative libertarians) find its impacts to be positive or neutral in most of these spheres, or believe that the "treatment" is worse than the disease. Meanwhile, those who seek change in current immigration policies (e.g., many state and local governments, organized labor, most black activist groups) point to the negative effects they believe current policies are imposing upon U.S. labor, minorities, and governmental programs.

Nor is it surprising that perceptions of costs and benefits tend to differ, depending upon the economic and political interests of the observer; the cross-cutting nature of such interests explains the sometimes bizarre alliances mentioned earlier. Those employers and economic sectors that have become dependent upon undocumented workers or find them a willing workforce with lower economic demands and unionization rates (e.g., fruit and vegetable growers in the Southwest and to some extent now in Florida; restaurant, hotel and sanitation services in the Southwest; garment manufacturers in Los Angeles and New York; and Southwest employers of low-skill construction workers) see them as essential for profitability.

The unemployed see them as competitors for scarce jobs. Those seeking to encourage unionization and improved terms of work see them as undercutting such efforts. State and local officials who find their local treasuries affected by additional demands upon such locally provided services as education, health, sewerage, police and fire protection, etc., see undocumented immigrants as a net drain on revenues. Others in government who are not required to finance additional expenses (e.g., federal officials, or local officials in areas with declining populations) may have a different perspective. As in so many other matters, where one stands often depends upon where one sits.

There is little doubt that the patterns of illegal immigration appear to have changed over the past decade. A high percentage of such immigrants are now moving to urban rather than rural areas of the United States, and a growing proportion are staying on for many years or permanently rather than returning home. There is also general agreement on two further points: that illegal migrants are eminently exploitable; and that although immigration is both an international and a national issue, the brunt of its fiscal effects is borne by local governments. For the latter reason, many local governments now see it in their interest to consider the international aspects of migration, and hence have been forced to become increasingly involved in debates about foreign policy insofar as they relate to migration flows. For example, both the National Association of Governors and the National Association of Counties have established formal committees concerned with foreign and immigration policies, and in recent years Southwestern governors have been meeting with their opposite numbers in Mexico to discuss economic and migration issues.

There is notably strong disagreement on the non-economic impacts of immigration trends, which include such matters as political participation, respect for law, and issues of language and culture.[16] Immigrants (especially those who are "illegal" or "undocumented") are seen both as threats to American political principles and institutions, and as reaffirmations of those same principles and of the flexibility of the American political system; as sources of increased criminality and disrespect for law, and as paragons of lawful behavior; as threats to the *unum* forged by free communication among citizens of diverse origin sharing a common facility in the English language, and as contributors to the *e pluribus* of cultural and linguistic diversity.

If anything, such "soft" areas of concern evoke greater emotion than do the issues of dollars and cents, as is evidenced by debates over the links between immigration trends and growing bilingualism in the United States. Fears (perhaps exaggerated) have sometimes been expressed that current trends may lead to destructive linguistic divisions in American society. Immigration patterns have contributed to organized opposition to the bilingual policies of federal, state and local governments. Examples include formation of a national advocacy group called U.S. English, chaired by former Senator S. I. Hayakawa; the strong public resistance (including a successful referendum campaign) in Dade County, Florida, to bilingual public policies promoted by Cuban migrants; and the passage in November 1984 of California State Proposition 38 entitled "Voting Materials in English Only," which attracted a 72 percent majority of 6.4 million votes after an initiative had collected over 600,000 signatures.

Although the number and impacts of current Latin American migrations to the United States are in dispute, there is less doubt about the pressures likely to arise over the coming decades. These expectations are based upon the daunting scale of labor-force growth projected for the major Latin American source countries over the remainder of this century.

As shown in Table 2, growth of the labor force in the 1960–80 period was high for most of these countries, ranging up ot 80–85 percent increases in Mexico, Colombia, and El Salvador, thus contributing heavily to serious problems of high unemployment, underemployment, and out-migration. Although the recent fertility declines experienced in some of the countries should result in moderating labor-force growth in the next century, inspection of Table 2 also shows that the International Labor Organization projections for the 1980–2000 period exceed even the huge increases of 1960–80. In relative terms, the projected increases expressed in percent

Table 2. Labor Force Increases, 1960–80 and 1980–2000

	Estimated/Projected Labor Force (In millions, rounded)			Absolute Increase		% Excess of 1980–2000 increase over 1960–80	% Change 1960–80	% Change 1980–2000
	1960	1980	2000	1960–80	1980–2000			
Latin America	70.8	117.1	207.3	46.3	90.2	95	+65	+77
Mexico	10.9	20.2	40.4	9.3	20.2	117	+85	+100
Colombia	4.9	9.0	17.2	4.1	8.2	100	+84	+91
Dom. Rep.	.9	1.6	3.2	.7	1.6	128	+78	+100
Jamaica	.6	.7	1.2	.1	.5	221*	+17	+71
Cuba	2.4	3.2	5.2	.8	2.0	136*	+33	+63
El Salvador	.8	1.5	2.9	.7	1.4	101*	+88	+93
Haiti	2.0	2.5	3.4	.5	.9	113*	+25	+36
USA								
(BLS-low)	69.6	106.9	130.1	37.3	23.2	-38	+54	+22
(BLS-med)	69.6	106.9	137.8	37.3	30.9	-17	+54	+29
(BLS-high)	69.6	106.9	150.0	37.3	43.1	+16	+54	+40

*Calculated on unrounded numbers due to small base.

Source: Data for Latin America from International Labour Office, *Labour Fource Estimates and Projections, 1950–2000* (Geneva: 1977), Volume III; for the U.S., Howard N. Fullerton, Jr. and John Tschetter, "The 1995 Labor Fource: A Second Look," *Monthly Labor Review*, 106 (1983), pp. 3–11. Detailed tables by personal communication.

are always higher for 1980–2000 than for the 1960–80 period. In absolute terms, the difference is even greater, exceeding 100 percent for most of the countries indicated. Most of them may nearly double the size of their labor forces in the twenty-year period. Labor-force realities of this scale clash profoundly with the capital-intensive development strategies being pursued in many Latin American countries. (The ILO projections were published in 1977, and revisions are much overdue. The projected increases might be reduced somewhat for countries like Mexico, which have experienced more rapid declines than expected in fertility over the past decade. But because most of the labor forces projected for 2000 had already been born in 1977, the magnitude of such revisions is likely to be small.)

The message is clear: Latin American countries that faced difficulties in the 1960s and 1970s in generating sufficient jobs for their growing labor forces can anticipate even greater challenges in the coming decades. To the extent that employment prospects affect pressures for out migration, the significance of such international movements is bound to increase.

4

Foreign Affairs and Latin American Migrations

As we have seen, concern about immigration has focused traditionally upon domestic considerations. Over the past decade, such concerns have been heightened, as evidenced by the major political debates stimulated by large-scale migrations from Latin America and Asia. Nonetheless, there are at least three important sets of foreign policy issues raised by Latin American immigration refugee movements: (1) the effects of foreign policies on Latin American migrations; (2) the consequences of these migrations for international relations; and (3) the use of migrations as tools of foreign policy.[17]

How Foreign Policy Affects Latin American Migrations

Clear illustrations of this linkage are provided by direct international interventions of a military or political nature that generate outflows of refugees or others seeking to avoid the consequences of the intervention. There are also cases of the converse—when interventions serve to restrain existing or potential outflows; or, put in another way, cases in which the absence of intervention can generate out-migrations as effectively as intervention itself.

Latin America provides examples of both effects. Indeed, in some cases nearly identical foreign policy arguments are being used to support utterly opposed foreign policy conclusions. For instance, proponents of current U.S. policies toward El Salvador and other Central American countries (including President Reagan and former Secretary of State Haig) have justified these policies in part by their restraining effects upon mass refugee outflows to the United States. They argue that such outflows can be expected to occur should leftist guerrilla forces be successful, and note that in the 26 years since the rise of Fidel Castro over 10 percent of the Cuban population has migrated to the United States.

Opponents of the Reagan Administration's policies in Central America argue the very opposite: U.S. support for El Salvador and opposition toward Nicaragua, they say, is increasing the levels of tension, violence and economic disruption that result in out-migration. In this view, out-migration can best be restrained through a reversal of American foreign policy, by establishing normal relations with Nicaragua and terminating economic and military support for El Salvador. (A corollary argument is that since U.S. foreign policy is responsible for out-migration from El Salvador and Guatemala, the United States has a moral obligation to grant refugee status to all such migrants, a position held by proponents of the church-related "sanctuary" movement.)

Foreign policy initiatives have also stimulated or facilitated non-refugee migrations from Latin America, sometimes unintentionally. For example, during both World Wars the United States negotiated bilateral agreements with Mexico for the provision of temporary workers. The World War II agreement developed into the so-called *bracero* program, and continued for nearly two decades after the war's end. The *bracero* program is generally agreed to have stimulated permanent legal immigration by temporary workers and their families who acquired permanent legal status, as well as illegal immigration by those who chose to migrate unlawfully along pathways and networks established by legal temporary workers.

El Salvador provides another example. Even the United Nations Secretariat, which must cautiously confine itself to describing only the official policies and pronouncements of its member-states, reports that as recently as the late 1970s the Salvadoran government was exploring the possibility of bilateral accords with such countries as Bolivia and Saudi Arabia to facilitate Salvadoran out-migration.[18]

Source countries of illegal immigrants have also sought to employ foreign policy instruments to facilitate or legitimize such flows. Typically these take the form of quiet diplomacy, but an unusually open example occurred in Mexico during final consideration of the Immigration Control and Reform Act of 1982 (the first version of the so-called Simpson-Mazzoli bill). Mexican political observers, who have long seen undocumented Mexican immigration as serving the interests of powerful employer groups in the United States, had expected the Simpson-Mazzoli bill to be blocked by an unlikely coalition of such employers and Hispanic activists. But when the bill passed the U.S. Senate overwhelmingly and was brought to the House floor, the Mexican Senate quickly adopted a strongly worded resolution on "this grave matter that negatively affects our good neighbor relations," and expressed its "alarm and concern for the repercussions which will impact both countries if the Simpson-Mazzoli legislation is passed." The resolution went on to characterize undocumented Mexican migration as a "transcendent matter [that] should not be considered from a unilateral perspective, but rather should be treated from a bilateral and even multilateral perspective," and to this end referred the matter to the foreign affairs organs of the Mexican Senate.[19] The resolution was not well-received in Washington, where it was seen by some as a flagrant attempt by a foreign power to intervene in the American legislative process.

In a recent issue of the journal *Foreign Affairs*, Mexican President Miguel de la Madrid H. attempted the difficult task of repeating such explicit criticisms of the pending U.S. immigration reforms while at the same time denying any intention to intervene in the U.S. legislative process:

> The situation of Mexican migrant workers in the United States has been, and continues to be, of special interest [to Mexico].

We have reiterated our support for the rights and interests of
Mexican nationals abroad. We have no intention of meddling
in the legislative processes of the United States. But we express
our concern over measures such as the Simpson-Mazzoli bill
which could affect the social, labor and human rights of numerous Mexicans, whose daily work and efforts represent considerable benefit to the U.S. economy.[20]

Similarly, in 1978 then-President José López Portillo met
officially with a group of nine Mexican-American leaders who
openly offered him their assistance in lobbying against the
Carter Administration's proposals to curb illegal immigration.
According to the Mexican-American participants, López Portillo told them "he was impressed and encouraged by the unity
of the Mexican-American movement, but that he had no intention of interfering in the internal affairs of the United
States."[21]

During that period and up to the present time, U.S. government officials have sought the reactions of the Mexican
government to immigration provisions that might affect Mexican migration to the United States, while avoiding any implication that Mexico might hold a veto power over U.S. decisions. Consistent with the de la Madrid and López Portillo
statements, Mexican government officials have regularly declined to enter into serious discussions of such matters, re-
serving the right to criticize but not consult. A typical ex-
change would include a Mexican statement acknowledging
the sovereign right of the United States to control immigration but urging concern for the human rights of Mexican undocumented migrants, followed by an American query as to
how the U.S. government can protect the human rights of
those living outside the purview of its legal system.

Finally, it is frequently argued that the most effective foreign policy instruments to restrain international migration lie
in the realm of foreign assistance, trade and/or direct investment. The goal is to accelerate economic development in
countries of out-migration through the more rapid creation
of jobs for those who might otherwise be impelled to seek
work abroad. But such proposals are afflicted with substantial

uncertainties as to the direction, size, and speed of their intended effects, as is discussed below in Section 5.

How Latin American Migrations Affect Relations Between Nations

The presence in a country of large numbers of nationals of another country almost inevitably affects the relations between the two states. On the one hand their presence may serve to deepen the level of understanding between the two countries, while on the other it may stimulate bilateral tensions, due either to the perceived mistreatment or exploitation of the migrants, or to the political activities of migrants against the government in control of their homelands. Either way, the effect is to focus the attention of the receiving country on the sending region. For the United States, the presence of nearly one million Cuban refugees and immigrants, many of whom are implacably opposed to the Castro government, has clearly made more difficult the regularization of U.S.-Cuban relations.

Sending countries also may seek to mobilize their expatriate or ethnically-related populations in support of their political relations with the host country. Often this occurs even without direct foreign "mobilization" efforts, as cultural, family and economic bonds lead to strong ethnic pressures on U.S. policies toward the countries of origin.[22]

Following the 1978 meeting between Mexican President López Portillo and Mexican-American leaders mentioned above, at which the latter offered Mexico their assistance in lobbying against immigration reform, the then-Chairman of the League of United Latin American Citizens (LULAC), Mr. Eduardo Morga, said to *The New York Times:* "We've never before told Mexico that we are all ready to help Mexico in the United States. We feel that in the future Mexico can use us as Israel uses American Jews, as Italy uses Italian-Americans, and so on." Since then, LULAC has emerged as one of the most active lobby groups opposing the Simpson-Mazzoli bill. Given the official Mexican criticism of the same legislation, described above, it is possible that the Mexican government accepted this open invitation to "use" Mexican-American lobby groups such as LULAC, although the similarity of their political opposition may also be a coincidental product of quite independent judgments.

Senator Charles Mathias (R-Md.), a leading member of the Senate Foreign Relations Committee, recently described as "plausible" the argument that immigration was the "single most important determinant of American foreign policy."[23] If true, the predominance of Latin Americans and Asians among recent U.S. immigrants represents an important force, among others, which over time may contribute to a redirection of American foreign policy toward Latin America and Asia and away from its traditional European focus.

Finally, migration flows may themselves be of sufficient concern to receiving countries as to affect their relations with the sending countries. This appears to have been the case with respect to U.S. policies toward Cuba and Haiti, and Venezuelan policies toward Colombia; similarly, Mexico's policies toward its neighbor Guatemala have been marked by concerns about Guatemalan migration into the sensitive regions of southern Mexico. A final, extreme example was the 1969 war between El Salvador and Honduras, known as the Soccer or Football War because of the catalytic role of a soccer match. This violent and destructive war had its origins in the illegal migration of large numbers of Salvadorans into the relatively prosperous lands of neighboring Honduras. Moreover, the Soccer War may have contributed both to the diversion of subsequent Salvadoran migration to the United States and to the civil war within El Salvador.

Latin American Migrations as Tools of Foreign Policy

When migrations are perceived as substantially in the service of foreign policy goals, they become foreign policy tools. Such uses of migrations have been made by both sending and receiving countries.

First, there is the explicit encouragement of out-migration to another country over which more political influence is desired. In some cases, civilian migration and settlement have been seen as instruments for asserting sovereignty or establishing de facto control over a contested area. For example, in the unsuccessful 1982 negotiations between Argentina and the United Kingdom that preceded the war over the Falkland/Malvinas Islands, the government of Argentina demanded as a condition for withdrawal of its troops that nationals of Argentina (1982 population: 28,600,000) be free to immigrate into the sparsely populated islands (population: 1,800). This demand reportedly was a major reason for the failure of the negotiations.[24] Over 150 years ago, the migration of Americans into what was then northern Mexico led eventually to the secession of the Texas Republic in 1836 and its admission to the United States in 1845.

More malevolently, mass expulsion of nationals (or even the facilitation of illegal migration by nationals of third countries) sometimes has been used to destabilize or embarrass adversarial neighbors. It seems likely, for example, that a desire to embarrass the Carter Administration is a partial explanation of the Cuban government's coercive inclusion of psychotics, terminally ill cancer patients, violent criminals, and other "scum" ("escoria" in Fidel Castro's description) in the 1980 boatlift, though there may also have been a desire to rid Cuba of the cost and bother of dealing with such people.

It has also been suggested that the Cuban influx included political and intelligence agents.[25] This unconfirmed possibility, the spy scandals in West Germany involving East German "refugees," and the recent arrests in California and New York of four Soviet and Czechoslovak "refugees" as alleged espionage agents do raise legitimate issues of national security. Of course, the United States is so permeable a society that the establishment of a foolproof identity for espionage purposes need not rely upon bogus "refugees." At a minimum, however, recent experience suggests that more attention will have to be paid to the risks of allowing refugees from Communist countries access to sensitive positions in government or industry.

Receiving countries have also made use of migrations as foreign policy tools. The admission of refugees from an adversary has often been seen as a means of discrediting that country and its political system. This use of refugee admissions has been especially popular in the United States with regard to out-migration from the Communist countries of Eastern Europe, as well as from the Soviet Union and Cuba. Similarly, many nations have admitted migrants from neighboring adversaries so as to sustain indigenous opposition to that country's government, in support of long-standing border disputes, or as human buffers against hostile military incursions. Sometimes support is provided for guerrilla operations, as in the Honduras-Nicaragua and Nicaragua-El Salvador cases.

The most obvious recent Latin American cases of such uses of refugee admissions have been in Central America. But Mexico and Cuba both have long provided a refuge and base of operations for anti-government exiles from such countries as Chile and El Salvador. Similarly, the United States has long offered refuge and in some cases active assistance for government opponents from Cuba, Haiti, and other Latin American nations.

Domestic advocates who oppose a given foreign regime also have often seen the admission of refugees from that country as a useful political tool in that their admission tends to discredit the regime in question. This amounts to the private use of a foreign policy tool also employed by governments, as noted above. The most active resort to such methods has been by private groups in the United States opposed to governments such as those of Haiti, El Salvador, Ethiopia, Cuba, Poland, the USSR, etc.

For example, Haitian political exiles and domestic groups opposed to the Duvalier regime have campaigned strongly in favor of political asylum for Haitian boat people on grounds that they face persecution and even death if returned to their homeland. Similar arguments undergird the church-related "sanctuary" movement, whose spokesmen often combine opposition to U.S. support for the governments of El Salvador and Guatemala with assertions that Salvadorans and Guatemalans returned to their countries face political persecution and death squads.

At the other end of the political spectrum, a coalition of conservative anti-Communist groups has recently initiated a campaign for more liberal refugee and asylum policies toward migrants from Communist countries. Their arguments from the political right bear a remarkable similarity to those from the left regarding Haitian and Salvadoran migrants. In the words of one of the leaders of the conservative campaign: "The State Department is 'selling out' defectors from communist countries and deporting them back to face human-rights persecution, concentration-slave labor camps, imprisonment and perhaps even death."[26]

U.S. policies have also engendered independent foreign policy activities by aliens that have proved difficult to contain. The training of the original Cuban assault forces for the unsuccessful Bay of Pigs attack against Cuba in 1961 implied a commitment by the United States to provide subsequent political asylum for the participants. For the past two decades, elements of these groups have been involved in clandestine activities—often without U.S. encouragement—against the Cuban regime. Some have become engaged with other immigrants from the Caribbean in the enormous, and dangerously damaging, narcotics trade centered in Miami, which the U.S. government has found very difficult to control. Miami also is a center for the recruitment of participants in the Nicaraguan "Contra" forces, who at some point—as with the Bay of Pigs forces—may also seek asylum in the United States. These in turn may then become part of a new generation of unofficial foreign policy entrepreneurs in the region, unintentionally generated by official U.S. policy.

5

Proposals for U.S. Policy Initiatives to Affect Latin American Migration Trends

Advocacy in support of U.S. policies to alter Latin American migration trends has ricocheted in all directions. At one time or another, arguments have been propounded for changes in immigration and refugee policies *per se*, U.S. policy in Central America, relations with Cuba, political and economic policies toward Mexico, and finally a broad range of economic, trade and investment policies.

Direct Immigration and Refugee Initiatives to Affect Latin American Migration Trends

Some serious proposals have been made to modify U.S. immigration and refugee policies in order to affect Latin American migration trends. Perhaps the simplest, and the most extreme, proposal is to have "open borders," i.e., to eliminate all immigration restrictions, especially for Mexico. The argument for such a policy is that, short of resorting to police state measures, immigration flows across the U.S.-Mexico border are impossible to control, and that in any case such migrations represent a positive contribution to American society. Hence in this view an open-borders policy is consistent with reality and with U.S. interests and values.

Most proponents of the policy appear to believe that total migration flows under an open-borders regime would not be as large as is widely believed—after an initial surge following the repeal of the immigration laws now in effect. Such arguments have not proved convincing in view of the profound poverty and the political problems that afflict many developing countries with large populations. Hence proponents of this extreme position are very few in number, consisting mainly of some ethnic and religious activists and libertarians.

A less extreme and more carefully argued proposal of similar complexion is that for a "North American common market." Under such a regime there would be unrestrained flows of goods, capital and labor between the United States, Canada, and Mexico, much as has been developed since World War II in the European Community of the highly industrialized countries of Western Europe. This approach evokes little or no support in the United States, where unlimited Mexican migration would be expected to affect adversely the U.S. labor force and to undercut U.S. producers with cheap Mexican produce and manufactures. Interestingly, the proposal until now has also received little support in either Mexico or Canada, where it has been seen as a way to open their markets and resources (especially energy) to unwelcome ownership and/or control by U.S. corporate interests. The 1984 election in Canada and the economic problems in Mexico may temper this kind of economic nationalism, though both Mexico and Canada seem unlikely to forget their long-standing concerns about political and economic domination from their neighboring superpower.

More limited proposals have been made for a regime of both free trade and unlimited migration within a restricted geographical area extending a specified number of miles into the United States and Mexico. These proposals have an initial attractiveness, until consideration is given to how controls would be applied to the movement of goods and people beyond the specified border area. In effect, such proposals amount to a limited movement of present controls back from current borders, but ultimately they do not resolve the boundary problems that arise when a highly industrialized nation shares a common border with a developing country or with a buffer region of intermediate development.

There have also been proposals that see control of illegal immigration as essentially a matter of direct border control, which would entail the expansion of the now-small Border Patrol and the construction of physical barriers along the U.S.-Mexico border. Extreme versions of such proposals have called for a near-militarization of the border, the polar opposite of the equally extreme proposals for an open border. Interestingly, these extreme border patrol models have sometimes been injected into the debate on immigration reform by opponents of immigration regulation, presumably to serve as strawmen to discredit any degree of enhanced enforcement.

More moderate proposals of this type urge the modest expansion and enhancement of border regulation, including the gradual expansion of the Border Patrol and the provision of adequate funds to update its antiquated detection, transportation and data processing equipment. Such incremental proposals have generated strong support in the Congress in recent years, with appropriations frequently exceeding those requested by the Executive branch.

Another set of proposals has achieved reasonable levels of support thus far; they provide for more than doubling the legal ceiling on Mexican immigration within overall U.S. limits on immigration. Such a proposal appeared in the late 1970s in the attractively-titled "Contiguous Neighbors Act of 1978" sponsored by Senator Kennedy, which was later incorporated into the Simpson-Mazzoli bill, twice passed by the Senate and once by the House of Representatives. The argument is that because of physical contiguity, Mexico and Canada deserve far larger immigration ceilings than do any other countries in the world. In addition, proponents argue that Mexico needs the out-migration "safety valve" for its high levels of unemployment and poverty, and that U.S. interests are thereby served by assisting Mexico's stable development. In both the

Kennedy and the Simpson-Mazzoli versions, the expected un-
derutilization of the greater number of visas available to Ca-
nadians (among whom there is no excess visa demand under
current ceilings) would be transferable to Mexico, where excess demand is obvious; the result would be very large increases for Mexico only.

Opinion differs sharply on the wisdom and justification for
such an exceptional provision of immigrant visas. Some critics
dispute the validity of the "safety valve" argument, noting that
the political systems in Mexico and other Caribbean countries
are far stronger and more sophisticated than is assumed.
Other critics point to the ambivalence in the sending countries themselves about continuing large-scale out-migration
to the United States, and note concerns about the "brain drain"
that would result from the continuation of uncontrolled immigration or from substantial increases in legal immigration.
Some see Mexico as a truly unique case, but others believe
that such special treatment is unjustified. One view here is
that long-term U.S. interests would be served best if Mexico
dealt with its own problems rather than exported them across
the border. Another view is that since much of the Caribbean
is as "contiguous" to the United States as is most of Mexico;
and since the small island nations of the region are far more
dependent on the migration "safety valve" than is Mexico, any
immigration preferences granted to Mexico must be extended to all of the countries of the Caribbean. In contrast, others
note that the geographical location of the Caribbean islands
makes them especially suitable candidates for the serious enforcement of U.S. immigration laws.

More generally, it is argued that the principle of international equity currently incorporated in the U.S. immigration
law should be retained as a matter of foreign-policy fairness
toward the rest of the world beyond Latin America and the
Caribbean. Since Mexico is already by far the largest single
source country and since Latin America and the Caribbean
constitute a very large source region for legal immigrants, any
further concentration of limited immigrant visas is seen, according to this principle, as not only inequitable but also
damaging to broad public support in the United States for a

continued generous policy toward immigrants and refugees. Moreover, the fact that Mexico and other states of the Caribbean region have relatively high per capita incomes is of concern to those who see increased international migration principally as a humanitarian policy aimed at providing economic opportunity for the poorest of the poor in the Third World.

A separate set of proposals is aimed not at the levels of permanent immigration, but rather is concerned with the provision of temporary foreign labor, for which Southwest agricultural interests have lobbied strongly. These "temporary worker" proposals have ranged from a limited streamlining of current legal provisions to open-ended admission of whatever number of workers is deemed necessary by employers. The various proposals have been opposed by organized labor and many minority groups, who see them as undercutting the hard-fought gains and protections achieved for domestic labor. The whole issue was an important one in the Congressional debates about the Simpson-Mazzoli bill wherein, by general agreement, agricultural interests mounted the most effective lobbying campaign. Recent press reports suggest that the Immigration and Naturalization Service may seek to liberalize the current H-2 temporary worker program via regulatory change in addition to legislation.[27]

Yet another set of proposals has favored the provision of "temporary refuge" (known in the inelegant terminology of U.S. laws as "extended voluntary departure") for all citizens from El Salvador (and sometimes for those from Guatemala, Haiti and elsewhere) who present themselves at the border or are already in the United States unlawfully or on temporary visitors' visas. The argument here is that such people are in jeopardy if they return to their violent and/or repressive homelands, and are therefore deserving of refuge as long as these conditions continue, especially given the U.S. political involvement in the countries in question. The implication of these arguments is that the United States now is obliged by international and domestic law to become a country of first refuge for persons fleeing violence and repression in their homelands, whether or not they have been admitted legally to the United States. Such arguments have been central to the church-related "sanctuary movement," which recently produced a number of arrests and convictions for violation of the immigration laws.

Opponents of the proposals for temporary refuge note that Salvadorans (and those from the other countries mentioned) have been emigrating to the United States and elsewhere for more than 30 years, long before civil strife erupted. They point out that El Salvador, as one of the poorest and the most densely populated nation in Central America, is a natural migration source country, and that in any case there is no justification for offering political refuge to the several hundred thousand Salvadorans who migrated illegally to the United States for economic reasons many years ago. Finally, they note that almost all Salvadorans and Guatemalans enter the United States after transiting Mexico, and should therefore seek refuge in that country first.

Unfortunately, advocates on both sides of this argument have tended to blur important distinctions among three categories of migrants: (a) those fleeing persecution on grounds of race, religion, nationality, membership in a particular social group, or political opinion, and therefore eligible for "refugee" status; (b) those fleeing the random dangers and economic dislocations of civil war and internal strife, and therefore *not* qualified for "refugee" status; (c) those seeking to escape poverty and find economic opportunity, and therefore properly seen as would-be "immigrants." The emotions aroused by this issue, especially given its perceived connections with American foreign policy, seem likely to generate continuing passionate debate in the coming years.

U.S. Policy in Central America

As discussed in Section 4, migration trends have been invoked in support of U.S. political or economic intervention to halt human rights abuses in such diverse countries as El Salvador, Guatemala and Haiti. The rationale for such interventions is that abuses by governments in these countries have led to refugee flight. These views are propounded by opponents of current Reagan Administration policies in Central America.

Ironically, the same intrinsic logic is also employed by supporters of U.S. policy in Central America and especially toward the Sandinista government of Nicaragua, from which tens of thousands of political opponents and Miskito Indians have fled. In this view, it is the failure of U.S. support for friendly states threatened by leftist insurgencies that will lead to mass out-migrations, with the outflows from Cuba since the 1959 revolution serving as the obvious example. The most alarming picture painted is of revolution spreading from Central America to Mexico, precipitating a flood of migrants into the United States numbering in the millions rather than the hundreds of thousands.

A fairer assessment than those offered by advocates on both sides of such debates is that no one knows (indeed, no one *can* know) which U.S. policy mix toward Central America will most effectively constrain outward migration flows. If current U.S. policies result in spreading violence and repression, as their critics believe, out-migration might well increase. If, on the other hand, U.S. policies lead to political stabilization and economic prosperity, as their proponents believe, out-migration might be restrained. To an outside observer, advocacy in this sphere appears to be a reflection more of one's general perspective on U.S. foreign policy toward Central America than of concern about migration trends as such.

U.S. Relations with Cuba

Proposals to limit diplomatic and economic ties with nations such as Cuba have been supported on sometimes contradictory grounds relating to Cuba's migration policies: (a) that the Cuban government has engaged in hostile and inhuman policies involving the mass expulsion of Cuban nationals to the United States; or (b) that Cuba has restricted the basic human right of its citizens to emigrate.

Similar (and equally contradictory) arguments have been marshaled in support of closer political and economic ties with Cuba on the grounds that the leverage achieved by such initiatives could be used either to deter repetitions of past mass expulsions, or to encourage more liberal emigration policies.

Once again, a fairer assessment would be that no one really knows what might be the impact on migration of alternative policies toward the Castro government. The Cuban case differs from that of Mexico in that it has involved past and future admissions of Cuban nationals as "refugees" and the reunification of families divided by migration. There is little doubt that part of the reason for U.S. admission of hundreds of thousands of Cubans as "refugees" from communism was to discredit the Cuban government. Such admissions have now been limited by the redefinition of "refugee" in the Refugee Act of 1980, discussed above.

Unfortunately, the migration issues between the United States and Cuba have been further complicated by Cuba's 1980 apparent expulsion of thousands of criminals, psychotics, and others who under U.S. law cannot be lawfully admitted, and Cuba's long-standing refusal to re-admit these Cuban nationals as required under international law.

In December 1984 the Cuban government agreed to re-admit approximately 2,700 of its citizens who are excludable from the United States in return for a U.S. agreement to reverse its freeze on legal immigration flows from Cuba. This agreement was followed by a stacatto series of interventions by the federal judiciary aimed at blocking repatriation of the excludable Cubans.

At the time of this writing (May 1985), all of these interventions have been reversed on appeal and the repatriation process allowed to proceed. This experience provides an ironic but not unique commentary on the problems for foreign policy that are posed by the division of powers under the U.S. Constitution.

Generally, a nation that values its bilateral relations with another country would not be expected to expel its "undesirables" and then refuse to re-admit them, recognizing that such actions would universally be seen as hostile. Thus it can be argued on the one hand that closer U.S.-Cuba ties should be sought as they would offer incentives to Cuba to assure that such unfriendly acts do not recur. On the other hand, the 1980 expulsion took place after several years' movement by the Carter Administration toward more normal relations with Cuba, including relaxation of travel restrictions, the establishment of Interest Sections, and bilateral agreements regarding fishing and navigation rights. Hence it can be argued that U.S. efforts to improve relations with Cuba might not be answered in kind, and indeed might invite another boatlift.[28]

Again, expectations in this regard are likely to be determined primarily by an individual's assessments of the Cuban government's intentions. If Cuba genuinely seeks better relations with the United States, it would be unlikely to hazard serious damage to such prospects by "encouraging" further mass migrations of the Mariel variety. But if the Cuban government's view of the United States is one of implacable hostility, such a policy might at some point again prove attractive for either domestic or foreign policy reasons.

Moreover, emigration from Cuba has generally fueled political forces opposed to normalized U.S.-Cuba relations. Many of those leaving Cuba have done so because of their dislike of the Castro regime. While Cuban-Americans often favor eased travel and immigration strictures, this has not translated into support for normal diplomatic relations between the two countries. Indeed, for many years a key consideration among Washington policy-makers addressing U.S.-Cuba relations has been the strong opposition of the Florida congressional delegation—pressed by the large and influential Cuban constituency in the state—to any moves toward normalization unless they are balanced by major changes in Cuban foreign and domestic policies. Cuba thus offers a major illustration of the direct linkage between immigration, domestic U.S. politics, and constraints upon U.S. foreign policy options.

U.S. Economic Relations with Mexico and the Caribbean

Unlike the Cuban case, concerns about migrations to the United States from Mexico and the Caribbean essentially involve efforts to control illegal or undocumented immigration, including both illegal entry across borders and violation of lawful temporary visas. The most obvious and direct means of dealing with such patterns are clearly the responsibility of the United States: more effective enforcement of U.S. immigration laws that are now allowed to be flagrantly abused. Such measures are matters of domestic policy and include direct law enforcement as well as indirect approaches to reduce the attraction of unlawful migration, such as the specific "employer sanctions" incorporated in the Simpson-Mazzoli bill or alternative deterrents proposed by its opponents. Generally, the provisions to discourage illegal immigration would make it unlawful for employers to knowingly hire illegal or undocumented aliens, with variations as to which employers would be covered, what penalties would be assessed, and how verification of legal status would be effected. Such measures tend to be supported by those seeking to control illegal immigration, and opposed by those favoring the status quo and/or fearing that such measures would lead to employment discrimination or government intrusions upon business.

While much of the debate has revolved around these domestic concerns, a number of foreign policy initiatives to deal with migration patterns have been proposed as alternatives (often by opponents of enhanced enforcement measures). The various proposals have included:

- increased American economic assistance focused on those developing countries that are major sources of international migrants ("source countries");

- reduction of tariff and non-tariff barriers limiting access of source country products to U.S. markets (proposals range from limited tariff reductions through to full-blown "common market" formulations);

- increased tax and other incentives for U.S. direct investment in source country economies.

The explicit goals are to accelerate job creation in source countries to meet their rapidly growing labor forces while at the same time raising incomes so as to reduce the economic incentives for out-migration. Proponents see such approaches as dealing with the problem "at its source" in the economic conditions prevailing in Latin America, rather than as a "symptom" experienced at the U.S. borders; as intrinsically humanitarian; and as politically attractive to those unwilling to support the direct regulation of immigration. Their proposals have special appeal for some members of Congress who wish to claim they support measures to restrain illegal immigration while at the same time appearing humanitarian and supportive of constituencies opposed to regulation of immigration.

Unfortunately, there are serious doubts as to the magnitude, the speed, and even the direction of the migration effects of such measures, be they in the form of concessional assistance, trade policies, or direct investment. The most pervasive doubt arises from the well-known difficulties in achieving sustained development. Economic and social development is a notoriously uncertain enterprise, depending fundamentally upon a whole range of uncontrollable and unpredictable factors, such as the weather, the availability or discovery of natural resources, trends in the world economy, and political stability. In particular, international assistance is of small magnitude compared to other economic flows affecting development.

Meanwhile, direct foreign investment often focuses upon capital-intensive technologies rather than on labor-intensive industries needed for rapid job-creation—in part because Latin American governments desire the transfer of the latest technology so as to begin producing goods that are competitive in the world market. Indeed, foreign investments made in labor-intensive but low-wage sectors such as cash-crop agriculture are often seen by Latins as "exploitation."

These circumstances illustrate the often ambivalent responses within Latin America to the expansion of U.S. aid, trade, and direct investment. More generally, the success or failure of development efforts is principally determined by the intentions and competencies of Latin American governing elites; without the active cooperation of such elites, a country like the United States can do little to promote more rapid job creation, more equitable income distribution, and reduced corruption and inefficiency.[29]

Development is not only uncertain; it is also a gradual process, with effects measured over the quinquennia and decades rather than the months and years. Thus even a successful development effort cannot be expected to have an impact upon migration trends in the near future.

Finally, even the direction of such effects is in doubt. The short-term effects may be opposite in direction from those of the long term. Although it may seem counterintuitive, most studies of migration and development conclude that successful economic and social development serves in the first instance to increase the pressures for both internal and international migration. By definition, to be effective such development must bring significant changes, indeed disruptions, in the established economic and social order. For example, improvements in the transportation and communication infrastructure can facilitate internal and international trade, but also encourage internal and outward migrations, as evidenced by the extraordinary urban growth rates in many rapidly industrializing developing countries.

The gradual improvements in opportunity that accompany economic development are necessarily marginal in size from year to year; they appear not to be large enough to reduce the relative attractiveness of opportunities elsewhere, but are of sufficient size to increase the ability to migrate. The migration-restraining effects of such development, if they do occur, seem to require much longer periods, and perhaps more substantial increases in economic well-being.[30] Empirically, some of the largest source countries of international migrants (e.g., Mexico, the Philippines, Taiwan, Korea, India) have been characterized by relatively successful development efforts with good growth records, and often substantial foreign assistance, foreign trade access, and foreign investment.[31]

The case of Mexico provides an object lesson in the uncertain impacts of economic development on migration patterns. During the post-World War II period, Mexico was one of the most rapidly growing economies in the world, until the onset of the economic crisis of the past several years. Over the same period, despite its rapid economic growth, Mexico experienced a large and growing migration, both internally to urban areas and internationally to the United States, where prevailing wages continued to be far higher. Even the exceptional growth of the Mexican economy in the 1970s did not reduce the magnitudes of internal and international migrations, both of which appear to have increased during the period.[32]

Although Mexico has long declined to accept direct development assistance from the United States, fearing greater economic and political dependency upon its northern neighbor, there have been many efforts to facilitate U.S.–Mexico direct investment and trade. Indeed, Mexico has been one of the largest recipients of direct investment from the United States: some $4 billion is now invested, concentrated heavily in manufacturing and accounting for 87 percent of the manufactured exports of Mexico.[33] For complex historical and psychological reasons, direct U.S. investment often stimulates fears of "dependency" in developing countries. In part for this reason, countries like Mexico have taken measures to restrict direct foreign investment in favor of foreign borrowing, in what has proved to be a mistaken belief that bank loans would lead to less dependency.

One of the best known agreements for the facilitation of U.S.-Mexico trade—the "maquiladoras" or "twin-plant" tariff arrangements of the Mexican Border Industrialization Program—offers further illustration of the sometimes unanticipated migration consequences of such economic policies. In brief, these agreements provide for the duty-free import into the heavily protected Mexican economy of unassembled components from the United States. The components are sent to regulated in-bond plants located mostly in Mexican border towns where they are assembled by Mexican workers who are paid at least the Mexican minimum wage, which is far lower than prevailing wages in the United States. The assembled products are then re-exported to the United States, which assesses duty only on the value added in Mexico, as allowed under Item 807 of the U.S. Tariff Schedule.

The major goals of the twin-plant program were to provide employment for Mexican workers within Mexico and relatively low-cost labor to participating American companies. In retrospect, the numbers of jobs involved have not been as large as is often thought, and the turnover rate has been high. More-

Table 3. Data on Selected Major Migration Source Countries, by Level of Income
(World Bank criteria)

	Population mid-1981 (millions)	GNP		Adult literacy, 1980 (%)	Life expectancy at birth, 1981 (in years)
		Per Capita, 1981 (dollars)	Average annual growth, 1960–81 (%)		
"Upper-middle" Income					
Mexico	71.2	2,250	3.8	83	66
Rep. of Korea	38.9	1,700	6.9	93	66
"Lower-middle" Income					
Taiwan*	7.0	1,400	5.5	82	–
Colombia	26.4	1,380	3.2	81	63
Dominican Rep.	5.6	1,260	3.3	67	62
Jamaica	2.2	1,180	0.8	90	71
Cuba	9.7	1,180	0.8	95	73
Philippines	49.6	790	2.8	75	63
El Salvador	4.7	650	1.5	62	63

Low Income					
Ghana	11.8	400	− 1.1	10	54
Sudan	19.2	380	− 0.3	32	47
Pakistan	84.5	350	2.8	24	50
Sierra Leone	3.6	320	0.4	15	47
Haiti	5.1	300	0.5	23	54
India	690.2	260	1.4	36	52
Nepal	15.0	150	0.0	19	45
Bangladesh	90.7	140	0.3	26	48

*Data for Taiwan are for 1978 and 1970–78.

Source: International Bank for Reconstruction and Development/World Bank, *World Development Report 1983* (New York and Oxford: Oxford University Press, 1983), Table 1.

over, there is concern that the location of the twin plants in Mexican border towns may have served to attract large numbers of people to these previously small urban areas, thereby exacerbating their urban problems and actually stimulating illegal migration over the easily crossed U.S. border.[34]

The preferential provision of aid, trade or investment for Latin American countries of out-migration also raises ethical concerns. U.S. foreign assistance policy has for many years been guided by the principle of directing assistance toward those countries most in need, while "graduating out" middle-income developing countries as their economies advance. For geopolitical reasons, both rationales have sometimes been honored in the breach in direct assistance allocations (e.g., the large assistance provided to strategic friendly countries), but U.S. support for such multilateral agencies as the U.N. Development Programme and the World Bank have emphasized the poorest-of-the-poor and graduation principles.

But most Latin American countries of out-migration are in the middle-income range and often have rapidly developing economies, and the migrants themselves are usually from the better-off but non-elite sectors of those countries. A quick inspection of Table 3 shows that many large migration streams to the United States come from relatively well-off countries such as Mexico, Colombia, Cuba, Taiwan, South Korea, and the Philippines; meanwhile migrants from the truly poor countries (such as Bangladesh, Nepal, India, Pakistan, Ghana, Sierra Leone, and Sudan) tend to gravitate toward the wealthier developing countries, especially the OPEC oil exporters. Even the poorest countries of Latin America like El Salvador and Haiti are relatively well-off compared to the poorest-of-the-poor, such as Bangladesh and Ethiopia.

Thus the proposed re-direction of aid, trade and investment toward Latin American countries of out-migration would raise some serious ethical issues that run counter to efforts to focus such transfers on those countries most in need. Trade preferences in favor of Latin American countries of out-migration, such as an expansion of those already incorporated in the Caribbean Basin Initiative,[35] would almost certainly lead to complaints of unfair treatment from other developing countries, particularly the four more advanced Asian developing countries (Taiwan, Korea, Singapore, Hong Kong) which already use over 50 percent of U.S. trade benefits under the General System of Preferences. (It might even, perversely, offer them incentives to encourage out-migration as a means of gaining more favorable treatment.) Incentives aimed at targeting private investment to specific countries are not likely to be successful except in marginal instances, and U.S. official efforts to encourage such investments in the past have not achieved noteworthy success.

Finally, it must be acknowledged that aid and trade initiatives are not likely to generate broad political support within the United States. The absence of a powerful constituency favoring foreign assistance is obvious and need not be discussed at length here. Proposals to open U.S. markets to Mexican and Caribbean products confront the political reality that most tariff and non-tariff barriers have been erected to protect powerful domestic economic interests which fear the competition of imports from Latin American countries with far lower wage rates. These concerns are held in common by both management and labor in diverse industries, including fruit and vegetable agriculture, the sugar and tobacco industries, textile producers, and the shoe and garment manufacturers. As a result of strenuous lobbying efforts by such groups, important Caribbean exports were excluded from the zero-tariff provisions of the Caribbean Basin Initiative.

Thus arguments that foreign assistance, trade or investment policies be employed to affect international migration trends require caution about their likely effectiveness and awareness of their ethical complications and political liabilities. Indeed, given the predominance of the U.S. economy in the Western Hemisphere, domestic economic policies adopted for reasons wholly unrelated to foreign policy or migration may have more profound effects than any of those discussed above. For example, the U.S. economic policies that have led to current high real rates of interest and the related strength of the dollar were adopted for wholly domestic reasons, but both have seriously constrained the capacity of many Latin American countries to generate employment for their growing labor forces.

The dollar debts entered into so enthusiastically in the

1970s turned out to be unmanageable burdens as the dollar appreciated dramatically against Latin American currencies and floating interest rates rose. The result has been financial crisis, slow or nonexistent economic growth, rising unemployment, declining real wages, and hence increased incentives favoring out-migration from countries such as Mexico, as already noted. In this arena, the United States has provided substantial emergency assistance, while at the same time supporting IMF efforts to assure forceful economic adjustment policies. These recent economic trends, coupled with lax U.S. immigration enforcement, go far toward explaining the apparent increases in illegal migration from Latin America and the Caribbean.[36]

There have also been some countervailing economic forces. The strong dollar has made Latin American exports cheap, thereby providing foreign earnings desperately needed to service past debts. Since oil export prices are denominated in dollars, Latin American oil exporters have obtained higher prices relative to their own currencies and to those of oil importers other than the United States. But overall, recent economic policies in the United States combined with Latin American borrowing policies in the late 1970s—both adopted for essentially domestic political reasons—have resulted unintentionally in increased pressures favoring international migration, both legal and illegal.

Multilateral Agreements to Regulate Migration

In recent years there has been a series of initiatives by migrant-sending countries, including some in Latin America, aimed at developing multilateral agreements about immigration. Most of these have focused upon the rights of migrant workers. Some are aimed at obtaining financial compensation for the loss of workers to migration. A few have focused upon the obligations of states not to create mass outflows of refugees.

In particular, the United Nations General Assembly in

1979 agreed to a Mexican government proposal to establish a working group on a new International Convention on the Protection of the Rights of All Migrant Workers and Their Families. The working group, chaired by a Mexican Ambassador, has been considering alternative draft proposals regarding the rights of migrant workers and their families and the obligations of sending and receiving countries. An initial Mexican draft sought to avoid distinctions between migrants who have lawful status and those who have entered illegally or violated the terms of their entry permits (what is called in U.N. parlance "migrants in an irregular situation"). A coalition known as the MESCA group, comprising traditional Mediterranean labor-exporters such as Italy, Spain, Greece, and Portugal and the Scandinavian nations Sweden, Finland, and Norway, has more recently submitted an alternative proposal that does make such a distinction by restricting the rights of those in an "irregular situation" to "fundamental human rights." By all reports, there has been little agreement within this U.N. working group, and its work has proceeded slowly.[37]

Migrant-sending nations have undertaken similar initiatives in the International Labour Organization (ILO). Their efforts culminated in ILO Convention No. 143, "Convention Concerning Migrants in Abusive Conditions and the Promotion of Equality of Opportunity and Treatment of Migrant Workers." The convention has not proved popular with labor-importing countries, and to date has been ratified by only a few countries, including Italy and Sweden.

Recently there have been further efforts within the ILO and the United Nations Conference on Trade and Development (UNCTAD) to adopt measures that would require labor-importing countries to provide financial compensation to labor-exporting countries. These derive from long-standing concern in some developing countries about the "brain drain" which results from emigration of some of their more creative and well-educated citizens, and the "brawn drain" of emigrating unskilled workers. The argument for compensation to migrant-sending nations is that the countries to which these people go are benefiting from their skills and labor, and therefore have an obligation to compensate the countries of origin for loss of their services and for investments in education, health, housing, etc., during the migrants' earlier lives.

Receiving countries such as the United States are unlikely to show much sympathy for this view, first of all because the right of the individual to migrate is well-established in international law[38] and has always been considered a fundamentally individual matter by most Americans. Moreover, migrants remit substantial sums over many years to families in their countries of origin, thereby contributing positively to the balance of payments and in some cases directly to government revenues. Finally, the establishment of values for such services as early education and health services is notoriously difficult, and the argument assumes that out-migrants would have found productive employment had they not departed their homelands, which often have high levels of unemployment and underemployment. For these reasons, it seems most unlikely that the proposals for compensation will find support among most countries of in-migration, though continuing advocacy by proponents should be anticipated.

On the refugee front, there have been two diplomatic efforts to negotiate multilateral agreements to restrain the mass outflow of refugees, such as those occurring in Indochina. The first of these was initiated by Canada in the U.N. Human Rights Commission, which appointed Prince Sadruddin Aga Khan (formerly High Commissioner for Refugees, and a popular candidate for U.N. Secretary General) to serve as Special Rapporteur. The report produced and distributed by Prince Sadruddin was unusually outspoken for a U.N. document and included three fascinating Annexes describing in some detail the conditions surrounding mass exoduses in a number of U.N. member-states (see excerpts below).[39]

Objections were raised by several states, reportedly including one important Latin American country, and the offending Annexes were expunged before final printing. (A blandly worded footnote in the expurgated version states that it was "Reissued for technical reasons.") One of the principal operational recommendations arising from the report was the establishment of an office of Special Representative of the Secretary General, charged with the explicitly political task of seeking to "avert, mediate, and/or forewarn" in settings that appeared to be moving toward mass outflows of refugees. To date, no concrete action has been taken in response to Prince Sadruddin's report.

The Federal Republic of Germany has also initiated an effort in the United Nations to formulate proposals to avert future mass exoduses. A "committee of experts" from 17 countries was established to consider possible proposals, but by all reports the effort proceeds only slowly.

It is possible that in the future the Organization of American States will become a forum for multilateral discussions of migration within the Western Hemisphere. Ultimately, however, all multilateral efforts must acknowledge that control over entry by non-citizens is a fundamental element of national sovereignty, despite the claims by some countries of out-migration that "higher principles" require continued free movement for their nationals into other countries. Any multilateral initiative that seeks to proceed without agreement on this basic matter of national sovereignty does not deserve to be taken seriously.

Some excerpts from Prince Sadruddin's report on human rights and mass exoduses:

> *On Afghanistan:* "This extraordinary exodus is the sequel of events in Afghanistan starting with the change from monarchy to republic, takeover by a regime with Marxist-Leninist leanings and the subsequent entry of foreign troops into the country. The reasons behind the upheavals in Afghanistan are to be found not only in the power play of foreign interests and influences and the imposition of an altogether alien system on a predominantly tribal Islamic society, but also in the socio-cultural fabric of Afghan society and political developments within the country during the last few years. . . .

"The Afghan population was not receptive to measures to bring about a classless society. Instead, viewing
the new government's ideology as incompatible with Is-
lam, and considering it dependent upon a foreign power,
it faced the Khalq with outbreaks of resistance as early
as the summer of 1978, and by a few months later a rural
uprising had erupted involving nearly all regions and
ethnic groups. After a year in power, Taraki's government had effective control only in towns and outposts
manned by concentrations of troops, and even then at the
cost of relying upon Soviet support."

On Haiti: "The first major wave in an otherwise unre-
markable migration from Haiti occurred after the election in 1957 of François Duvalier, the father of the present President, whose repressive methods became well
known beyond the confines of the island. Those who left
then were members of the middle class who had no economic mobility in the feudal order of that period—doc-
tors, lawyers, engineers, teachers, other professionals
and broad segments of the urban middle class. The more
recent migratory wave consists mainly of simple peas-
ants, whose position has become untenable because their
livelihood has been eliminated in the expropriation of
huge areas of land by the large-scale mechanized plan-
tations increasingly transforming the face of the island."

On Ethiopia: "In the seven years which have elapsed
since a military takeover changed the political face of the
Ethiopian empire and put it on the path of socialism,
events so devastating have occurred that millions of people have been internally displaced or have fled to surrounding countries."

On Mexico-to-U.S. migration: "While the majority of Mexicans are apparently quite content to remain at home, the
combination of under-provision of jobs, high inflation
and an appreciable income disparity with Mexico's northern neighbour leads large numbers to a point that they
are ready to cut their ties with home, at least temporari-
ly, to try their chances in the United States. Many of
these who leave are reportedly farmers who brought in

little more than $500 a year working on an "ejido" (government-owned smallholding) and who know through the Hispanic information network that they can expect to earn $150 per week in the United States. . . .

"In practice, the cost-of-living [sic] differential combined with the propensity of accompanying younger family members to assimilate may mean that he never returns home. Studies have shown that many employers in the United States actively seek to employ Mexicans, knowing not only that they are generally prepared to work long hours for low pay in jobs largely shunned by U.S. citizens, but also that they do not air grievances, being loyal and anxious to please. . . .

"Analysts suggest that immigration and particularly illegal immigration help to maintain the rate of profit for those agricultural and non-monopoly sectors of capital which are incapable of drawing on the mechanisms open to monopoly capital for maintaining an adequate level of surplus."

Source: United Nations, Commission on Human Rights, *Study on Human Rights and Massive Exoduses*, E/CN.4/1503, 31 December 1981, Annex II.

6

U.S. Foreign Policy and International Migration: Interests and Goals

Whereas in the past international migration issues could safely be considered marginal to foreign policy, they have now entered squarely into its province.[40] Mass movements of people across international borders can now fairly be described as both consequences and causes of potentially dangerous domestic and international tensions. Migrations now also appear to be regarded by some states as handy tools of foreign and domestic policy. For the United States, these connections have special meaning in its relations with Latin America and the Caribbean.

While migrations have thus inextricably entered the hard world of *realpolitik*, it must never be forgotten that migrants are not mere instruments of state power, but human beings—flesh and blood—whose lives are sometimes in severe jeopardy and whose rights are often abused. These hazards are especially marked for *bona fide* refugees. Because refugees' lives are placed in risk by their own governments, they both deserve and receive special international attention beyond that due to more traditional migrants, who continue to be entitled to the protection of their governments.

American foreign policy should be sensitive to this unusual combination of vulnerable human lives and *realpolitik*. A sensible set of goals for such policy include the following:

1. Refugees and Asylum

A fair but strictly enforced policy on the acceptance of bona fide refugees must be followed.

This goal requires a continuing willingness to provide protection and generous assistance to those qualifying as *bona fide* refugees, both those in countries of first asylum and those permanently resettled in the United States. It also means a firm decision to forego temptations to "stretch" the refugee designation. In the past, U.S. policy has often yielded to this temptation by offering resettlement as refugees to those motivated primarily by economic or family reasons (and hence properly viewed as would-be immigrants). Such admissions under the refugee category have in part been humanitarian in intent, but have also been used to embarrass adversarial source countries (e.g., Cuba) or in response to political pressure from domestic interest groups. Ironically, such "flexibility" in U.S. policy has had the unintended effect of stimulating further migrations by those who do not support the regimes in power, thereby relieving their governments of political dissidents. It has also blurred important distinctions between refugees and other migrants, and thereby encouraged other domestic pressure groups to lobby for their "refugees."

Recent attempts to manipulate the refugee and asylee designations have been so considerable that these high-minded concepts are in danger of utter debasement. If this does occur, those genuinely entitled to their special protections will find the door closed. Resistance to such abuses need not deny applicants for refugee and asylum status impeccably fair and expeditious adjudications. Advice from the State Department, the only government agency with first-hand knowledge of the political circumstances in countries of origin, can be helpful to this end. Beyond the purely informational role, it is legitimate to take foreign policy issues into account in determining which of the world's millions of refugees should be offered permanent residence in the United States, for it is obvious that the granting of asylum can have foreign policy implications (as was demonstrated by the recent awkward experience with a tennis player from the People's Republic of China). Nonetheless, care must be taken to prevent crude foreign policy determinations of what are essentially humanitarian concerns that must be dealt with objectively on a case-by-case basis.

A country such as the United States, which self-evidently attracts large illegal migrant flows for primarily economic reasons, is inviting further abuse of refugee and asylum provisions if it offers such status to large national groupings irrespective of the merits of individual claims. This applies equally to countries of origin as diverse as Cuba, Nicaragua, El Salvador, Haiti, Vietnam, Guatemala, and Poland.

Due to characteristics of its political and economic system, the United States is not well-suited to provide first asylum or temporary refuge. First asylum requires that other nations be willing to provide third-country resettlement, and that their offers be accepted by those given first asylum. The evidence from past experience is that most other countries are not prepared to resettle refugees already admitted to the United States, except for a few sparsely populated developing countries that are unacceptable to the persons involved and, on occasion, a few Western nations prepared to accept small numbers for symbolic reasons. Providing temporary refuge requires the willingness and capacity to terminate the temporary status once circumstances in the home country improve. But the well-known ability of small but committed interest groups to control policy issues, coupled with the exceptionally litigious and slow-paced American legal system, suggest that such "temporary" refuge in the United States would in many cases become a backdoor approach to permanent residence.

2. Mass Outflows

Concerted attention must be given to emerging trouble spots in the Americas that could result in mass expulsions of citizens by authoritarian governments of the right or the left, or in mass outflows of migrants or refugees.

Over the past decade, mass outflows have occurred from countries in the region as diverse as Haiti, Cuba, El Salvador, Nicaragua, Guatemala, and Mexico. In many cases such movements have threatened both the lives of the migrants and the stability of countries experiencing mass influxes. Special attention should be paid to countries that have engaged in mass expulsions of their own citizens, such as Cuba's expulsion of "undesirables" in 1980. Negotiations for the return of these Cuban nationals began that same year, and have only recently begun to bear fruit; but contingency plans also should be in place to deter any Cuban consideration of similarly hostile and inhumane actions.

More generally, the United States should employ the full array of foreign policy instruments to deter would-be expellers and to contain future mass exoduses. These instruments should include all pertinent political and economic pressures exerted via bilateral, third-country and multilateral routes. There should also be careful contingency planning for the use of police and other forces, including those of the U.S. Coast Guard, to deter future mass migrations by boat. Future circumstances may arise in which even more vigorous efforts, involving the National Guard and other military units that were deployed for law enforcement purposes during the civil rights movement in the 1960s, may be required to demonstrate U.S. determination to exercise its sovereign right to regulate entry across its borders. Several legislative proposals for such "immigration emergencies" have been introduced and deserve careful scrutiny.

If such deterrence efforts prove unavailing, consideration should be given to denying offending governments the benefits of membership in the international system, such as access to the facilities of the International Monetary Fund, the World Bank, the Inter-American Development Bank, and so on. Such efforts, while difficult, would emphasize that nations expelling their own citizens offend against fundamental principles of the international system of sovereign nation-states.

The recommendations discussed above for a Special Representative of the U.N. Secretary General concerned with mass exodus situations also warrant attention; the new office would have a mandate to undertake the political tasks involved in averting mass exoduses, tasks that cannot be handled by existing international agencies such as the avowedly apolitical

U.N. High Commissioner for Refugees. This recommendation for a political approach to the inhumanity of mass exoduses is worthy of scrutiny, notwithstanding legitimate American disenchantment with other elements of the United Nations system.

3. Economic Policies

Despite the ambiguous evidence already noted, policies should be explored that might assist in reducing the economic and other incentives to unlawful international migration from countries in Latin America and the Caribbean.

The possible economic measures include scrutiny of foreign assistance, trade and investment policies insofar as they might contribute to labor-intensive economic development in source countries over the very long term. It should always be recognized that contrary effects may be experienced in the shorter term, that the impact of economic measures depends heavily upon government policies in the sending countries, and that such measures are no substitute for direct U.S. efforts to regulate immigration effectively and humanely. While the effects of successful development may not restrain (indeed may stimulate) out-migration over the short and medium terms, in the long run international migration pressures will continue to increase unless productive employment can be generated for the rapidly growing labor forces of Third World countries. Moreover, assistance to these countries in accelerating their development has many other strong arguments in its favor, however uncertain its impact may be on out-migration.

In addition to such efforts, greater attention should be paid to the significance of domestic U.S. economic policies for Latin American economic development. Fiscal and monetary policies that contribute to high interest rates and an overvalued dollar clearly have exacerbated the debt problems faced by many Latin American countries, notwithstanding the fact that much of their debt burden may have arisen from unwise policy choices. Such concerns add to an already overwhelming set of arguments in favor of containing the U.S. deficit, coupled with constructive and sensitive American support for IMF efforts to encourage more balanced fiscal and monetary policies in the debtor nations.

4. Coherence, Humanity, Enforcement

It must be made clear to Latin American governments and peoples that the United States welcomes legal immigrants and refugees subject to the provisions of U.S. law, but that it will no longer allow either widespread illegal immigration or the exploitation of illegal aliens to continue.

To date, the most balanced and effective proposals in this direction have been those incorporated in the Immigration Reform and Control Act of 1983 (the second Simpson-Mazzoli Bill), which achieved widespread political support and only narrowly failed passage during the final days of the 98th Congress. The proposed legislation includes several significant initiatives: the de-legalization of the knowing employment of illegal aliens ("employer sanctions"), including appropriate verification procedures; the legalization of substantial numbers of resident illegal aliens; the streamlining of existing programs enabling agricultural employers to obtain sufficient harvest labor; and the gradual enhancement of direct border and interior enforcement of immigration laws.

The last of these provisions, enhanced enforcement, appears to have no open opponents. Of the other elements, the one drawing the most broad-based opposition was the proposal to legalize the millions of illegal aliens who have been resident since 1981. Conservative political groups opposed this provision as rewarding illegality with eventual citizenship and voting rights, and state and local governments refused to support it unless they were guaranteed 100 percent reimbursement of all costs incurred when millions of illegal aliens gain legal rights to their services. It seems likely that future proposals will incorporate delayed or more restricted legalization provisions, though ultimately some form of legalization will be needed at least for those who have lived unlawfully in the United States for many years.

The proposal that led to the most intense lobbying by narrower interest groups was the one to deter the employment of illegal aliens through employer sanctions. While politics often makes for strange bedfellows, the alliances here were stranger than on almost any other political issue. For example, the most vocal lobby groups opposing employer sanctions included politically conservative or libertarian groups, especially those representing the economic interests of large employers of illegal aliens (e.g., the Western Growers' Association, the California Farm Bureau, the California Tree and Grape Fruit League, operating under an umbrella organization called the Farm/Labor Alliance). Aligned uncomfortably with them were three liberal activist groups (the League of United Latin American Citizens (LULAC), the Mexican-American Legal Defense and Education Fund (MALDEF), and the American Civil Liberties Union. Supporters of employer sanctions included generally liberal organizations such as the AFL-CIO and the National Association for the Advancement of Colored People (NAACP).

In the end, none of the groups opposing employer sanctions was able to develop credible alternatives to such deterrents in the workplace, and hence broad political support for employer sanctions appears to be in place. One indicator of this is the recent submission of a bill incorporating a form of employer sanctions (H.R. 30, 99th Cong., 1st Sess.) by Representative Edward R. Roybal, one of the most implacable congressional foes of employer sanctions throughout the past four years of debate.

If, in the end, comprehensive and balanced reforms continue to be blocked by interest groups, attention will have to be given to a more piecemeal approach. Initial steps would likely include increased border enforcement, enhanced interior enforcement such as workplace and neighborhood "sweeps," and other direct measures.

There would be considerable international support for more effective U.S. immigration laws, as similar problems of growing illegal immigration are causing concern in much of

Western Europe, in Canada, and even in developing countries such as Mexico, Venezuela, Nigeria, India, Nepal, and Hong Kong. Strong criticism should also be anticipated, especially from certain Latin American countries that over the past two decades have come to rely upon out-migration as part of their implicit development policies. But such criticism is likely to be limited to the short-term period of adjustment. Over the longer term, there is little likelihood that a more effective U.S. immigration policy would poison relations with any Latin American country, especially if such measures also serve to reduce the levels of exploitation experienced by Latin American migrants.

Exploitation of migrants has caused emotional political criticism in source countries such as Mexico. Hence, serious efforts to control such abuses would, over the longer term, contribute to improved U.S.-Latin American relations, and warrant energetic attention. However, even the most sincere efforts to halt maltreatment cannot be effective unless the magnitude of the vulnerable population can be reduced to manageable levels, and until those whose rights are abused are willing to come forward to file complaints.

5. Increased Foreign Policy Attention

There is now an overwhelming case for more serious and concerted attention to Latin American immigration and refugee matters at all levels of the foreign policy process.

Ultimately, issues as fundamental to national sovereignty as the control over entry by non-citizens cannot be viewed as mere bargaining chips in the foreign policy arena. In the United States, as in most other countries, immigration and refugee policy has always been under the jurisdiction of domestic policy organs such as the Judiciary Committees of Congress and the Department of Justice. Since domestic concerns are and will continue to be predominant, it would be unwise to suggest that immigration and refugee issues now belong principally within the apparatus of foreign policy.

Nonetheless, the foreign policy connections to international migration have now grown to sufficient magnitudes to warrant closer and better-informed attention within the geographic and functional bureaus of the State Department, in the National Security Council, in the Defense Department, in agencies dealing with international trade and investment, and in the many congressional committees that oversee these executive functions.

The immigration effects of U.S. foreign policy actions are often slow and difficult to anticipate. Because the consequences may be "down the track" three or five or ten years, policy makers rarely focus on the issues involved as they consider day-to-day matters. The future migration of hundreds of thousands of Indochinese refugees to the United States was in no one's mind while the Vietnam War policy was being developed. The prospect of hundreds of thousands of Cubans migrating to the United States was not a prime issue when policy toward the Cuban revolutionary government was being formulated in 1959–61. Although prospective migration has become an issue on both sides of the debate about the United States' Central America policy, it is unclear whether it is perceived as a real or straw issue by opposing groups.

The case is strong, even overwhelming. The important foreign policy implications of immigration and refugee movements, and the converse effects of international relations upon the movement of millions of people, require that increased attention be paid within the foreign policy sector to issues hitherto seen as largely domestic. These issues have now become so central to a broad array of foreign policy concerns, and to the life chances of so many people, that more concerted and sensitive attention can only serve to improve both the effectiveness and humaneness of American foreign policies.

Notes

1. United Nations, *Concise Report on the World Population Situation in 1983* (New York, 1984), p. 62.

2. It should be emphasized that these are projections, not predictions. While the methodology employed is statistically conservative, urban areas of such sizes are literally off the scale of all human experience—the largest urban areas today are less than 18 million—and so the projections might not occur for reasons that cannot be anticipated.

3. U.S. Committee for Refugees, *World Refugee Survey, 1984* (New York, 1984), pp. 37–41.

4. Philip L. Martin and Marion F. Houstoun, "European and American Immigration Policies," *Law and Contemporary Problems*, 45(2), 1982, p. 29. See also United Nations, Economic and Social Council, "Recommendation of the Expert Group on Population Distribution, Migration and Development," E/CONF.76/PC/7, 27 July 1983, para. 40.

5. The old definition appears in the Immigration and Nationality Act, Section 203(a)(7) (repealed), of which the full text is as follows:

> (7) Conditional entries shall next be made available by the Attorney General pursuant to such regulations as he may prescribe and in a number not to exceed 6 per centum of the number specified in section 201(a), to aliens who satisfy an Immigration and Naturalization Service officer at an examination in any non-Communist or non-Communist-dominated country, (A) that (i) because of persecution or fear of persecution on account of race, religion, or political opinion they have fled (I) from any Communist or Communist-dominated country or area, or (II) from any country within the gen-

eral area of the Middle East, and (ii) are unable or unwilling to return to such country or area on account of race, religion, or political opinion, and (iii) are not nationals of the countries or areas in which their application for conditional entry is made; or (B) that they are persons uprooted by catastrophic natural calamity as defined by the President who are unable to return to their usual place of abode. For the purpose of the foregoing the term "general area of the Middle East" means the area between and including (1) Libya on the west, (2) Turkey on the north, (3) Pakistan on the east, and (4) Saudi Arabia and Ethiopia on the south: *Provided*, That immigrant visas in a number not exceeding one-half the number specified in this paragraph may be made available, in lieu of conditional entries of a like number, to such aliens who have been continuously physically present in the United States for a period of at least two years prior to application for adjustment of status.

The new definition, incorporated in the Immigration and Nationality Act, Section 201(42), was drawn from the U.N. Convention Relating to the Status of Refugees of 1952 and its associated Protocol of 1967.

6. This section draws upon two useful background papers prepared for the Council Study Group: Dale Frederick Swartz and Saskia Sassen-Koob, "Migration and Foreign Policy," October 1983; and Dennis Gallagher, "United States Refugee Policy and Latin America," February 3, 1983.

7. Mary M. Kritz, "International Migration Patterns in the Caribbean Basin: An Overview", in Mary M. Kritz, Charles B. Keely, and Silvano M. Tomasi, *Global Trends in Migration* (New York: Center for Migration Studies, 1981), p. 210.

8. Kritz, p. 226.

9. Adriana Marshall, "Structural Trends in International Labor Migration: The Southern Cone of Latin America," in Kritz et al., p. 241.

10. Kritz, p. 226.

11. Marshall, p. 241.

12. Swartz and Sassen-Koob, p. 24.

13. Immigrants entering over land borders or arriving by ship via cabin class were not included in these counts, but their numbers are unlikely to have been very large.

14. Kritz, p. 214.

15. Immigration and Naturalization Service, *Statistical Yearbook 1980*, Table 13.

16. For a discussion of such issues, see Lawrence H. Fuchs, "Immigration, Pluralism, and Public Policy: The Challenge of the Pluribus to the Unum," in Mary M. Kritz, *U.S. Immigration and Refugee Policy* (Lexington, Mass.: Lexington Books, 1983), pp. 289–316. See also Michael S. Teitelbaum, "Right Versus Right: Immigration and Refugee Policy in the United States," *Foreign Affairs*, Fall 1980, pp. 41–44.

17. For a discussion in greater depth of the links between immigration/refugee movements and foreign policies, see Michael S. Teitelbaum, "Immigration, Refugees, and Foreign Policy," *International Organization*, 38(3) (Summer 1984), pp. 429–450.

18. United Nations, *International Migration Policies and Programmes: A World Survey* (New York: 1982), p. 17.

19. Reprinted in U.S. Congress, *Congressional Record*, December 17, 1982, p. H10256.

20. Miguel de la Madrid H., "Mexico: The New Challenges", *Foreign Affairs*, Fall 1984, pp. 69–70.

21. *The New York Times*, February 12, 1978.

22. Less conventional efforts, such as the use of expatriates for terrorism or sabotage, may also be used, but these appear to be more characteristic of the Middle East (e.g., Libyans in Europe, Palestinians and Iranians in the Persian Gulf, etc.) than of the Western Hemisphere.

23. Charles McC. Mathias, Jr., "Ethnic Groups and Foreign Policy," *Foreign Affairs*, Summer 1981, p. 979.

24. *The Times* (London), 22 July 1982. Examples from other world regions include the 1975 "peaceful 'march of conquest'" by 350,000 unarmed Moroccan civilians into the disputed territory of the former Spanish Sahara, and the West Bank settlements policy pursued by successive governments of Israel since the 1967 war.

25. Georges Fauriol, "U.S. Immigration Policy and the National Interest," Immigration Policy Paper #2, Center for Strategic and International Studies, Georgetown University, December 8, 1983, p. 32.

26. *The Washington Post*, February 15, 1985, p. E1.

27. *The New York Times*, January 27, 1985.

28. It is worth noting in this regard that the 1980 Cuban influx was not halted by actions of the Carter Administration; it was terminated by the Cuban Government.

29. Thomas K. Morrison, "The Relationship of U.S. Aid Trade and Investment to Migration Pressures in Major Sending Countries," *International Migration Review*, 16(1), Spring 1982, pp. 4–26; also Sidney Weintraub, "U.S. Foreign Economic Policy and Illegal Immigration," *Population Research and Policy Review*, 2 (1983), pp. 211–31.

30. Weintraub, pp. 218, 226.

31. Morrison, p. 15. See also Nelle W. Temple, "Migration and Development: A Preliminary Survey of the Available literature," *Staff Report of the Select Commission on Immigration and Refugee Policy, Appendix B* (Washington: 1981), p. 206.

32. Weintraub, p. 226.

33. Morrison, p. 22.

34. Agency for International Development, "The Relationship of U.S. Aid, Trade and Investment to Migration Pressures in Major Countries of Origin," *Staff Report of the Select Commission on Immigration and Refugee Policy*, Appendix B (Washington: 1981), p. 11.

35. The Caribbean Basin Initiative does not favor labor-intensive economic sectors; on the contrary, labor-intensive products such as sugar and textiles were excluded from preferential access to U.S. markets for domestic political reasons.

36. For an analysis of similar data for the 1970s, see David North, "Enforcing the Immigration Law: A Review of the Options," *Staff Report of the Select Commission on Immigration and Refugee Policy, Appendix E* (Washington: 1981), pp. 269–374.

37. See United Nations General Assembly, Thirty-Eighth Session, Third Committee, "Report of the Open-ended Working Group on the Elaboration of an International Convention on the Protection of the Rights of All Migrant Workers and Their Families," A/C.3/38/5, 11 October 1983.

38. "Everyone has the right to leave any country, including his own,

and to return to his country." Universal Declaration of Human Rights, Article 13(2).

39. United Nations, Commission on Human Rights, *Study on Human Rights and Massive Exoduses*, E/CN.4/1503, 31 December 1981, Annexes I and II.

40. See Aristide R. Zolberg, "International Migration and Foreign Policy: When Does a Marginal Issue Become Substantive?" in Center for Migration Studies, *In Defense of the Alien*, Vol. VI, 1983.

Suggested Readings

International Migration Review, *Irregular Migration: An International Perspective*, Special Issue, Volume 18, Fall 1984.

A useful set of recent articles. This is the only journal devoted to research on international migration, and other volumes are also worthy of inspection.

Kritz, Mary M., Charles B. Keely, Silvano M. Tomasi, editors, *Global Trends in Migration: Theory and Research on International Population Movements* (New York: Center for Migration Studies, 1981).

A valuable and well-organized compendium of articles with a broad international perspective.

Miller, Mark J. and Philip L. Martin, *Administering Guest Worker Programs: Lessons from Europe* (Lexington: Lexington Books, 1982).

An informative discussion of European experience with "guest worker" policies, with a useful set of appendices including relevant international conventions, treaties, accords and procedures.

Select Commission on Immigration and Refugee Policy, *U.S. Immigration Policy and the National Interest*, Final Report of Select Commission, reprinted as Joint Committee Print by U.S. House of Representatives and U.S. Senate, Committees on the Judiciary, 97th Congress, 1st Session, (Washington: August 1981).

Essential reading for anyone interested in U.S. immigration and refugee policies. One of the more impressive examples of the Select Commission genre.

Select Commission on Immigration and Refugee Policy, *Staff Report, Appendices A through H*, April 1981.

A rather mixed collection of materials commissioned by the Select Commission, some of very high quality, others quite mediocre.

A valuable compendium of what otherwise would have become a fugitive literature.

U.S. Committee for Refugees, *World Refugee Survey, 1984* (New York: American Council for Nationalities Service, 1984).

An authoritative and balanced annual source on current circumstances in the refugee sphere.

U.S. Congress, Congressional Research Service, *Selected Readings on U.S. Immigration Policy and Law*. A compendium prepared for Senate Judiciary Committee, 96th Congress, 2nd Session, October 1980.

A worthwhile compilation of materials otherwise difficult to find.

U.S. House of Representatives, Select Committee on Population, *Legal & Illegal Immigration to the United States* (Washington: December 1978).

An early congressional analysis of U.S. immigration issues, with special attention to the quality of available evidence.

Study Group on Latin American Immigration and U.S. Foreign Policy

Daniel A. Sharp, *Chairman*
Susan Kaufman Purcell, *Director*
Helen Drusine, *Rapporteur*

About the Author

Michael S. Teitelbaum was educated at Reed College and Oxford University, where he was a Rhodes scholar. His academic appointments in demography have included Assistant Professor and Faculty Associate of the Office of Population Research, Princeton University and University Lecturer in Demography and Fellow of Nuffield College, Oxford.   He has also served as Staff Director of the Select Committee on Population, U.S. House of Representatives, and on the professional staffs of the Ford Foundation and the Carnegie Endowment for International Peace. Presently he is Program Officer at the Alfred P. Sloan Foundation in New York.

His publications include numerous articles in journals such as *Population Studies, Foreign Affairs,* and *Science,* and two recent books: *The British Fertility Decline: Demographic Transition in the Crucible of the Industrial Revolution* (Princeton University Press, 1984) and, with J. M. Winter, *The Fear of Population Decline* (Academic Press, 1985).

Recent Publications of the Council on Foreign Relations

A Changing Israel, Peter Grose, Vintage Books/Random House, 1985.

Prospects for Peace in the Middle East: The View from Israel, Presentations made at a conference held in cooperation with The Dayan Center for Middle Eastern and African Studies, Tel Aviv University, Council on Foreign Relations, 1985.

Ripe for Resolution: Conflict and Intervention in Africa, I. William Zartman, Oxford University Press, 1985.

Technological Frontiers and Foreign Relations, Anne G. Keatley, editor, National Academy Press, 1985.

Arms and the African: The Military Influences on Africa's International Relations, William J. Foltz and Henry S. Bienen, editors, Yale University Press, 1985.

American Hostages in Iran: The Conduct of a Crisis, Warren Christopher, *et al.*, Yale University Press, 1985.

Canada and the United States: Enduring Friendship, Persistent Stress, John H. Sigler and Charles F. Doran, editors, Prentice-Hall, 1985.

Third World Instability: Central America as a European-American Issue, Andrew J. Pierre, editor, Council on Foreign Relations, 1985.

For complete catalog and ordering information please contact Publications Office, Council on Foreign Relations, 58 East 68th Street, New York, N.Y., 10021, (212) 734-0400.